The Evoluti Intelligence

CU00687759

Inner World Explained

Introduction

Welcome to the exploration of the depths within existence. Life's tapestry is woven with threads of understanding, determination, conflict, and curiosity. As we embark on this voyage, we invite you to delve into the inner realms of human experience. Together, let's demystify the teachings that have shaped our understanding of ourselves, our thoughts, and the world around us.

Within these pages lie profound tales of human growth, resilience, and transcendence. Each story acts as a portal into the intricacies of our consciousness, offering insights into the relationship between our physical being and the intangible realms of ideas, emotions, instincts, and quests.

"The Birth of Cognition" takes us back to time as we encounter Wonder—an inquisitive ape—and witness her extraordinary journey that led to cognitive thinking. Through Wonders perspective, we unravel the enigma behind thought and recognize how our physical bodies play a pivotal role in shaping our intellectual abilities.

In *"The Rise of the Subconscious Mind," we* are immersed in an exploration of self-identity and optimism that endures over time. Join us as we embark on a captivating adventure alongside the character, diving deep into the depths of self-discovery. We navigate through a maze of uncertainties and self-doubts, ultimately embracing the power of self-love and resilience.

"The Rise of Consciousness" takes us on a journey where our senses and impulsive instincts engage in an ongoing battle for control. This symbolic tale uncovers the timeless conflict between our desires and rational thoughts as we strive for heightened awareness and understanding. It sheds light on the paths we tread in search of balance, offering an exploration of human consciousness awakening and the choices we make along this transformative path.

"The Journey into Ultimate Space" propels us into the cosmos, following a lone explorer's quest for enlightenment and understanding. Through this odyssey, we delve into spirituality, philosophy, and the boundless spirit within humanity that transcends our limitations.

As you delve into these stories, we extend an invitation to you to explore the teachings that have shaped humanity's evolution, determination, and spiritual pursuits. Let's together illuminate these teachings and bring them to light.

These stories are crafted to not only enlighten but also inspire drawing from the rich tapestry of human experiences to uncover the intricate workings of our inner worlds. Get ready for a captivating journey of thoughts, emotions, and exploration where each story reveals an aspect of the human mind. Join us as we unravel the wisdom that has shaped our understanding of ourselves and the universe, aiming to forge a stronger connection with the fundamental truths that govern our existence.

Welcome to a realm where storytelling acts as a doorway to self-discovery, reflecting the complexities of our paths. Through these narratives, we aim to shed light on the path toward enlightenment and encourage you to embark on your journey of self-reflection and discovery. Let's begin these stories as we delve into the realms and demystify the teachings that anchor us to our true essence.

Contents

Story 1: The Birth of Cognition

In ancient Body's realm, a dream did spring
Where Wonder's curious heart took wing
Cognition's birth, a tale untold
In Humana's journey, wisdom unfold.

Chapter 1: Introduction

In the twilight of prehistoric times, in a land untouched
by recorded history, lay the mysterious kingdom of the
body. It was a world brimming with life enigmas and
the relentless pursuit of survival—a domain where
nature's rhythms governed every occurrence. Around
17,000 BC, amidst this expanse, a story brimming with
curiosity and profound significance was about to be
etched into the annals of evolution.

At its core stood a character whose name would echo
through time—Wonder. Wonder was no inhabitant of
the body; she was an ape driven by unparalleled
curiosity that would soon transcend her ordinary
existence. Until that fateful day arrived, her life had
been dictated by routines. She wandered through
landscapes with her belly swollen in anticipation of
new life—an emblematic symbol amidst an ever-
changing world caught in perpetual flux. Like her
companions, she searched for food, enjoyed the warmth

of the sun, and sought shelter beneath trees when darkness fell upon the world. However, Wonder stood out from the rest due to her curiosity, which sparkled in her eyes. A thirst for knowledge set her on a path of exploration. Mere existence didn't satisfy her; instead, she yearned to comprehend the essence of her being. Her unrelenting pursuit of knowledge foreshadowed a transformation—an evolution of thought and consciousness that would reverberate across time.

In the following words, we will embark on a journey into Wonders being. Delving into the mysterious epoch of 17,000 BC and exploring the depths of her extraordinary curiosity We will bear witness to a dream that will forever alter the course of her life—a dream destined to set in motion a series of events aimed at unravelling the mysteries surrounding cognition.

In a world where survival was paramount, the emergence of cognition was an improbable phenomenon. In this cauldron, the Wonders tale unravelled, bringing forth the story of a realm that would undergo everlasting change due to the emergence of awareness.

Chapter 2: Wonder's Ordinary Life

Wonder led a life that followed the usual rhythms of existence, much like the other inhabitants of the Kingdom of Body. She belonged to a group of apes, a tapestry woven with threads of survival, instinct, and kinship. Within this group, Wonder had a seemingly unremarkable place.

Her journey into the extraordinary began with her pregnancy, a phase that marked a turning point in her life and set the stage for the transformative events that would follow. In those times, pregnancy symbolized continuity and represented the eternal cycle of life. It was a time when the kingdom's future was entrusted to mothers like Wonder, who carried within them the promise of life.

As she traversed through the landscapes of the kingdom, Wonders rounded belly became a symbol of hope and perpetuation for her clan. She wasn't alone in this experience; other female apes shared in the journey of motherhood, each carrying within them cargo that represented future generations. It demonstrated their species enduring legacy against nature's laws.

Within the community, Wonder held a position that may not have stood out at first glance. She was a member of a knit clan where strong bonds were formed through shared experiences of gathering food, finding shelter, and caring for their young. Her interactions with her apes were characterized by the simple yet profound rituals of communal life. They moved together in harmony, guided by the instinctual wisdom passed down from one generation to another.

Under the surface of this seemingly ordinary existence, Wonder possessed a unique curiosity that set her apart. While her peers focused primarily on survival needs, she viewed the world with a different lens. Her inquisitive nature burned within her like a flame, yearning to comprehend the world beyond meeting basic necessities. The rustling leaves whispered secrets to her. I enticed her to delve into the mysteries concealed within their domain.

During her pregnancy, Wonders role within the clan became more significant. She now carried not only responsibility for herself but also for nurturing another life growing inside her. It was a duty she wholeheartedly embraced, committed to ensuring the clan's survival and prosperity. As she traversed the landscape, her actions were driven by more than instinct; they carried a deeper sense of purpose. When she sought nourishment, Wonders choices went beyond satisfying her hunger; they were focused on providing the sustenance required for her growing offspring. Her instincts guided her. Even in their early stages, her consciousness played a role in these decisions. It reflected the cognitive processes that would later define her remarkable journey. Throughout her pregnancy, Wonders interactions with members of her clan were marked by a strong sense of communal harmony. The apes supported one another, sharing resources and offering protection while collectively nurturing their young. It was a world where the bonds of kinship were tightly woven together, where the survival of everyone was inherently tied to the survival of all.

In the tranquil embrace of the Kingdom of Body nestled beneath trees, the protective shadow of Wonders voyage represented merely a small thread in the vast tapestry of existence. Her pregnancy symbolized hope. Played an integral part in the kingdom's perpetual dance between life and survival. She had no idea that her normal life, her position in the group, and the future she held inside her would soon collide with something. This would set off a series of events that would change her life forever. The dream that awaited her would be a turning point, revealing the secrets of understanding and leading to a transformation beyond what's usual when embarking on an incredible journey.

Chapter 3: The Dream That Changed Everything

Under the night sky, adorned with countless twinkling stars, Wonder's dream unfolded like a tale whispered by the universe itself. In this dream, she embarked on a journey that transcended the boundaries of the ordinary and forever altered her path. In the depths of her slumber, Wonder experienced an event—the birth of a being unlike any she had ever encountered. This was no birth; it was a revelation of something truly extraordinary. As she cradled the newborn in her arms, Wonder bestowed upon her the name Humana—a name that resonated with the essence of humanity.

What immediately distinguished Humana from members of their ape clan was evident to all who saw her. Despite having four limbs like everyone else, she possessed two arms and two legs—an embodiment of her uniqueness. It was a sight for Wonder, as this distinctive trait held promise for something profoundly different. Humana's physical attributes, distinct from others, hinted at an entirely new form of existence. Her two legs offered the potential for movement—a mode of mobility that set her apart from her fellow apes. Her two arms, with their dexterity, appeared ready for activities that went beyond the usual tasks of gathering and climbing that characterized the everyday life of the clan.

In Wonders Dream, this extraordinary birth wasn't a biological occurrence; it represented something remarkable. It showcased the power of evolution and stood as evidence of endless possibilities lying dormant within the genetic makeup of the clan. Humana's physical form became a canvas onto which limitless potential was painted, foreshadowing change in a world where change was scarce and valuable.

As Wonder cradled Humana in her dream, she experienced a sense of awe and curiosity mirroring her waking life. It felt as if this dream child embodied the questions that had danced within Wonder's mind— questions about existence, the potential for transformation, and the enigmatic nature of consciousness. The dream wasn't merely a tale; it held significance. It hinted at the interplay between physicality and cognitive capacity—an enduring theme that would resonate throughout history in the Body Kingdom. In this dream scenario, Wonder had given birth not only to human but also to seeds of cognition— subtle beginnings hinting at a new way of thinking and perceiving the world.

As Wonder emerged from that dream, she carried with her a mixture of wonder and excitement. The boundaries between what's ordinary and extraordinary seemed blurred. Her curiosity, once confined to the depths of her thoughts, now had a canvas on which to delve into the enigmatic aspects of existence. In the waking world, as Wonder observed her fellow primates, she couldn't. Ponder over the nature of her dream and the significance of Humana's distinct physical characteristics. Little did she realize that this dream was not a fanciful flight of imagination but rather an introduction to a journey that would unravel the mysteries surrounding cognition. It would be a journey guided by the qualities possessed by her dream child, Humana.

Chapter 4: The Unusual Evolution of Humana

As Humana grew, her development took a path that distinguished her from her peers in both subtle and profound ways. Her journey was like a woven tapestry intertwined with curiosity, unconventional thinking, and behaviors that defied the norms of her ape clan.

In the realm known as the body, where apes lived in the present moment, guided by instincts and immediate needs, Humana stood out like a shining star against a dark night sky. She displayed peculiar behaviors and thought processes that left her mother Wonder puzzled, while her fellow apes were bewildered and sometimes even afraid.

One of the remarkable differences between Humana and other apes was her inclination to contemplate the world around her. While her peers were content with survival-focused routines, like hunting for food and seeking shelter, Humana's mind was constantly engaged in reflection. She pondered not only the world as a source of immediate resources but also as an intricate network of interconnected phenomena. Her contemplations created ripples in the waters of consciousness, reaching outward to touch upon the very essence of existence itself.

As her peers searched for food, it appeared that she was on a quest to understand, exploring the reasons and methods behind the world surrounding her. Observing the interactions among her apes, Humana couldn't help but notice overlooked patterns and subtle nuances. She observed how their actions were guided by instinct and their responses were driven by survival needs. It seemed as if they were actors in a play following a script written by nature itself. However, for Humana, this script felt incomplete. She questioned the motives behind their actions. I needed to uncover the underlying causes propelling them.

Her curiosity led her into the realm of contemplation, an uncharted territory within the realm of the body. This shift in thinking resulted in peculiar behaviors that set her apart from her clan. While her peers were satisfied with maintaining things as they were, Humana began experimenting with approaches to problem solving. She would explore techniques for hunting, gathering food, and constructing shelters, often leaving her fellow apes bewildered.

One day, as she ventured into the foliage of their habitat, Humana's mind overflowed with thoughts that surpassed mere survival needs. She found herself contemplating the idea of being unique, wondering why she stood out from the rest. Her curiosity, like an unyielding stream, flowed through her mind. "Why am I so different from everyone?" she pondered to herself. "Why am I capable of thinking while they are not? Perhaps it is a gift inherited from our ancestors or maybe bestowed upon me by the divine. "These questions swirled in her thoughts like leaves caught in a breeze.

As she observed her arms, a realization struck her with sudden clarity. "No, it cannot be," she reflected. "Arms are physical, while the mind is intangible. They exist as entities." However, the more she contemplated it, the more she entertained the notion that her arms held the key to her abilities. This revelation would forever alter her understanding of herself. Humana recognized that her arms had been involved in tasks and endeavours that demanded thinking, planning, and adaptability.

Over time, their constant usage had compelled her to think in ways that others did not. With her arm dexterity and ability to manipulate objects, Humana's arms became the driving force behind a revolutionary form of intelligence—a cognitive brain. While her fellow apes relied on instincts and basic bodily reactions, Humana's arms became the foundation where thinking came to life.

This newfound understanding sparked a wildfire in Humana's mind, illuminating the mystery of her uniqueness. She realized that her transformation into a thinker, planner, and being with abilities was not bestowed upon her by divine intervention or ancestral favouritism. Rather, it was the result of her tireless work and contemplation through her arms, shaping her into an unparalleled creature within the realm of living organisms.

As Humana regained her senses, filled with joy and tranquillity, she knew that this was only the beginning of an extraordinary journey. The peculiar behaviours she exhibited, thoughts she pondered, and evolution of her cognitive brain were not isolated incidents; they heralded a new era in the realm of living organisms. It was an era where cognition wasn't an elusive dream but rather a tangible reality—all thanks to Humana's curious expedition as an ape.

Chapter 5: Wonder's Puzzlement and Humana's Curiosity

Wonder, the leader of the ape clan, found herself constantly puzzled. As she watched her child, Humana, grow and develop, a mix of confusion and concern overwhelmed her. Humana's unique qualities became increasingly apparent, making Wonder contemplate the mysteries surrounding her offspring.

When Humana was born, Wonder experienced the joy any mother would feel. She cradled her baby in her arms with love and an innate protective instinct. Little did she know then that this fragile infant would embark on a journey of curiosity and self-discovery that would challenge their ape clan's existence.

As Humana matured, her physical features started distinguishing her from apes. While the rest of the clan displayed traits like sturdy bodies, sharp senses, and instinctive behaviors, Humana possessed distinct peculiarities that were impossible to ignore. Her limbs and her arms exhibited exceptional dexterity and agility, which allowed her to manipulate objects with unmatched precision among their clan.

The newfound dexterity Wonder saw in Humana immediately captivated her. It was truly astonishing to see her effortlessly reach for fruits up in the trees, displaying a remarkable grace and finesse that seemed almost otherworldly. The rest of the ape clan could only watch in awe their nimble limbs, unable to match Humana's natural ability to gather sustenance.

However, Wonder's initial amazement soon turned into confusion. She couldn't fathom how her daughter had acquired extraordinary physical traits. The other apes in their group exhibited the characteristics that had been passed down through generations: strong limbs for climbing, keen senses for detecting danger, and basic survival instincts. Humana seemed to possess something beyond the ordinary.

As Wonder continued to observe Humana's behaviour, her confusion deepened. While the rest of the clan focused on their activities like foraging, grooming, and playing, Humana stood out with an insatiable curiosity that bordered on obsession. She would spend hours meticulously examining objects, turning them over in her hands, lost in thought, as if contemplating the essence of the world around her. Initially dismissing these behaviours as childhood curiosity that would fade over time as Humana matured, Wonder soon realized that her daughter's curiosity was not merely a passing phase but a defining characteristic.

Humana's curiosity only grew stronger with each passing day, setting her apart from the rest of the clan in many ways. As Wonder observed her daughter's blossoming inquisitiveness, worry began to creep into her thoughts. She couldn't. Ponder whether Humana's exceptional qualities were a gift or a burden. Would her daughter's extraordinary talents pave the way for greatness? Would they isolate her from the clan, turning her into an outsider in a world where conformity was paramount for survival?

While Wonder wrestled with these uncertainties, Humana's curiosity continued to deepen. She found herself questioning herself, not the world around her. Also, her own existence. Why was she different from others? What purpose did her unique abilities serve? These questions took root in her mind like seeds planted in soil, fuelling an unwavering drive to seek answers.

Humana's curiosity burned within her like a flame, illuminating the mysteries of her being. She longed to comprehend the world, unravel the depths of her individuality, and decipher the enigma of her prowess. She had embarked on a journey to explore herself—a journey that would have profound consequences for the Ape clan and the entire kingdom of the body.

Chapter 6: The Mystery of Being Unique Humana

A being with an extraordinary sense of individuality, grappled with profound questions that echoed through the corridors of her curious mind when she found herself in the heart of the ancient realm called Body, surrounded by lush forests and under the timeless expanse of the sky. As she observed her apes and contemplated the striking differences that set her apart, one question overshadowed all others: why was she unlike them?

Humana's contemplation about her distinctiveness became the central focus of her existence. It was a question that consumed her waking moments and infiltrated her dreams. She had viewed the world through the perspective of her apes, witnessed their instinctive behaviours, and marvelled at their aptitude for navigating life's challenges.

Yet she keenly recognized that she possessed dissimilarities. Unravelling the enigma behind her capacity to think was a puzzle that captivated Humana's longing. While members of her clan relied on instincts and acquired behaviours for survival, Humana's mind resembled a labyrinth filled with thoughts, ideas, and inquiries. She pondered over the mysteries surrounding her abilities, delving into the inner workings of her mind that allowed for introspection, reasoning, and contemplation.

As Humana sat beneath the canopy of trees, surrounded by the gentle whispers of the forest, she often found herself lost in contemplation. She pondered whether her capability to think was a blessing or a curse. Did it grant her an advantage in comprehending the world around her, or did it isolate her from others? The answers eluded her like flickering fireflies beyond her grasp. Her thoughts weaved a tapestry of questions. She entertained the notion that her distinctiveness was not happenstance but an intentional design, a purpose waiting to be revealed.

During moments of introspection, Humana would gaze at her own hands with wonder. She recognized that they were more than tools for survival; they were instruments for exploration and discovery. Her hands enabled her to manipulate objects to create and express herself in ways beyond the comprehension of apes.

Her ability to think critically, reason logically, and communicate through gestures and sounds set her on a path of self-discovery. With these abilities, she embarked on an experimental journey to convey her thoughts and ideas to members of her clan. Their reactions varied from curiosity to confusion as they struggled to comprehend the profoundness of her intellect.

Humana's contemplation extended beyond her immediate surroundings. She gazed up at the night sky, marvelling at the bodies that adorned it with their radiant presence. Her mind wandered into the cosmos, pondering the stars and planets that gracefully danced in the expanse above. Her thoughts transcended the boundaries of the forest, reaching out towards the unknown with a thirst for knowledge.

However, with each question she posed and every reflection upon her uniqueness, Humana's feeling of solitude deepened. She yearned for a connection, for a soul who could fathom the depths of her musings. She longed to share her discoveries, her queries, and her aspirations with another being who could peer into the recesses of her mind.

Chapter 7: The Role of Arms in Shaping Thoughts

In the realm of the ancient kingdom of the body, while the world around her continued its timeless rhythms, Humana experienced a profound moment of revelation. This moment would forever transform her understanding of her uniqueness and set her on a path of exploration that would reshape the fate of her clan.

As Humana gazed at her hands, delicately tracing the lines on her palms with her fingers, she was struck by a realization akin to lightning piercing through a stormy night. It was an epiphany that illuminated the core of her existence—her arms served as catalysts for her extraordinary cognitive abilities.

In this transcendent instant, Humana comprehended that her arms were not extensions solely meant for grasping and manipulating objects. They were conduits through which her mind connected with the world. Channels through which she navigated and interacted. Her arms had been companions throughout a journey filled with exploration and adaptation, compelling her to think critically, strategize, and adjust in ways distinct from other members of the primate family. From infancy onward, Humana have been engaged in tasks and activities that demand thinking, reasoning, and adapting to environmental challenges. They had become her means of survival and her tools for exploration. She remembered the occasions when she reached for ripe fruits hanging high in tree branches, stretching her arms and calculating the perfect angle to ascend. Each successful grasp showcased her ability to plan and execute movements, a skill that distinguished her from others.

Her arms also served as instruments for crafting, allowing her to create tools and implements that extended her capabilities. They enabled her to fashion weapons for hunting and self-defence, thereby enhancing her adaptability in a world full of challenges. However, it wasn't the physical aspects of her arms that influenced her cognitive abilities. They were involved in processes such as problem-solving.

It seemed as though physical tasks required thinking, which in turn demanded more thinking. She came to realize that her arms had shaped a kind of cognitive brain that had evolved in response to the demands of the physical world around her. With this understanding, a sense of clarity washed over Humana.

She no longer viewed her uniqueness as an enigma or a peculiar quirk of nature. Instead, she saw it as the outcome of interactions between her arms and her mind a beautiful synergy that had given rise to her ability to think. Her arms had been the catalyst for her transformation into a thinker, a planner and a being with capabilities that made her distinct from other apes. This realization filled her with wonder and gratitude because she knew that her abilities weren't a result of intervention or luck but rather the fruits of her own efforts and experiences.

As she continued to ponder the role played by her arms in shaping her cognitive development Humana's sense of isolation gradually faded away. She no longer felt alone in possessing abilities because she understood that her fellow apes also possessed their own distinct traits and skills each shaped by their interactions with the world around them.

With this newfound perspective Humana rejoined her clan feeling a sense of belonging and purpose in her heart. She was no longer an outsider but an integral part of the tapestry that was their ape community. She shared these revelations, with clan members using her enhanced abilities to communicate and teach.

Chapter 8: The Birth of Human Cognition

As I, Humana, continued to contemplate the significance of my arms in my journey, I delved deeper into the origins of my cognitive abilities. It was a voyage of self-discovery that unveiled the impact my arms had on my mental development, ultimately leading to the emergence of my cognitive brain.

During moments of contemplation, I traced back the beginnings of my cognitive evolution to my earliest interactions with the world. It was through engaging my arms in activities that I felt a stirring within me, awakening an entirely new realm of possibilities.

From a tender age, I keenly explored my environment. My arms served as conduits for me to touch, manipulate, and explore objects surrounding me. Whether it was feeling the texture of a tree's bark or delicately touching flower petals, these tactile sensations fed invaluable sensory information into my developing mind. These experiences formed the foundation upon which I began to comprehend and grasp the world around me.

As time went on and I grew older, my arms became tools for interacting with everything around me. They enabled me to reach for sustenance, climb trees with nimbleness, and even create tools. Each action necessitated coordination along with planning and problem-solving skills. Her arms served as the means by which she transformed her thoughts into actions.

A pivotal moment in her growth occurred when she started creating tools. Using rocks and branches, she fashioned implements that allowed her to access new food sources and protect herself from predators. This act of toolmaking required not only physical skill but also creative thinking and problem-solving abilities.

Furthermore, her arms played a role in her social interactions. Through gestures and movements, she communicated with apes, sharing information and emotions. Her arms became a means of expression, fostering the development of language skills and social connections within her group.

However, the remarkable aspect of her arms was their contribution to abstract thinking. As she tackled complex tasks, her mind was challenged to envision solutions and anticipate outcomes. Her arms acted as a bridge between her thoughts and the physical world, allowing her to experiment and learn from her experiences.

Ultimately, it was through this interplay between thought and action that abstract thinking emerged a defining characteristic of cognitive development. Her arms empowered her to explore, adapt, and innovate, honing her abilities through countless trials and errors in response to the demands of both the physical environment and her determination to thrive.

The immense influence of her arms on her growth cannot be emphasized enough. Not only did they contribute to her survival, but they also played a crucial role in unlocking the potential for advanced thinking. Her cognitive abilities flourished thanks to the collaboration between her arms and her mind.

Chapter 9: Humana's Return to Reality

In the beginning, Humana felt a sense of isolation and difference from the apes due to her newfound cognitive abilities. She struggled to express her thoughts and ideas, often leading to misunderstandings with her clan. They couldn't fully grasp the depth of her insights. Understand the significance of her actions.

Over time, Humana managed to bridge the gap between herself and her clan. Through gestures and simple demonstrations, she conveyed her intentions and shared her knowledge. Gradually, her fellow clan members began recognizing how special she was. Started appreciating the value she brought.

A pivotal moment in Humana's journey to reality came when she realized that her cognitive abilities could greatly benefit her clan. She observed their struggles in life, whether it was finding food or protecting themselves from predators. With this understanding, she devised innovative solutions for these challenges.

For example, she introduced the concept of using tools to her clan, teaching them how to create implements for hunting and gathering. Although there was hesitation among some members, they soon realized that these tools were practical and started adopting Humana's methods. The improvement in their efficiency and survival skills became evident.

Humana's ability to plan and strategize played a role in ensuring the well-being of her clan. She had a knack for foreseeing dangers and coming up with strategies to avoid them. By understanding predatory behaviour, she guided her clan away from conflicts and towards hunting grounds.

As Humana's fellow clan members witnessed the advantages of her cognitive abilities, they gradually embraced her as an esteemed member of their community. Instead of isolating her, they celebrated her unique qualities and appreciated the valuable contributions she made to their collective survival.

Humana felt a sense of belonging and purpose within her tribe as she returned to reality. Acceptance brought happiness and a deeper understanding of humanity. She took joy in making a positive impact on the lives of her fellow apes. Witnessing her clan thrive through her efforts filled her with satisfaction.

Moreover, interacting with her tribe members provided Humana with a sense of connection. Camaraderie that she had longed for. She discovered the beauty of shared experiences and the warmth that comes from connections. This realization went beyond cognitive abilities; it was a testament to the significance of social bonds and finding one's place in the world.

Chapter 10; Impact on the Kingdom of Body

As Humana shared her knowledge and insights with her clan remarkable changes started occurring in the kingdom of Body. The adoption of tools and the development of thinking led to significant progress in their ability to secure food protect themselves from predators and adapt to changing environments.

One of the notable consequences of Humana's journey was a higher survival rate for her clan. With her guidance they became skilled hunters and gatherers ensuring a continuous supply of sustenance. This not improved individual clan members health and wellbeing but also allowed their population to flourish.

Previously survival, in the kingdom of Body was a struggle where each day presented new challenges and dangers. However, Humana's cognitive abilities introduced an adaptability and resilience.

The clan quickly learned how to anticipate and handle dangers resulting in fewer casualties and a greater sense of safety. Additionally with the emergence of thinking the social dynamics within the clan underwent a significant shift. They began to appreciate the contributions made by Humana fostering a spirit of cooperation and shared goals. Together they became more efficient at collaborating pooling their combined knowledge and skills to tackle challenges as a united group.

This newfound collaboration went beyond survival necessities. Clan members started sharing stories and experiences passing down wisdom from one generation to another. Language evolved from communication to convey intricate ideas and concepts. The development of a shared language played a role in preserving and transmitting knowledge leading to cultural growth throughout the kingdom.

Humana's journey also deeply impacted the clan's spirituality and sense of self identity. They started contemplating the mysteries of their surroundings reflecting on their existence and pondering the forces that governed their lives. With abilities now within reach they delved into philosophical inquiries and explored abstract notions.

As their understanding of the world expanded, they felt a connection, with nature and the wider cosmos. They developed customs and traditions to pay homage to the rhythms of existence the shifting seasons and the enigmas of the cosmos. The realm of Physicality underwent a revival embracing a newfound respect, for the interdependence of every living creature.

Chapter 11: The Significance in the Context of Human Evolution

The incredible journey of humans and the emergence of the brain hold great importance when considering the broader scope of human evolution. In this chapter, we will delve into the connections between human history and the development of thinking, highlighting similarities that shed light on how our cognitive abilities have evolved.

Humana's journey mirrors humanity's collective journey towards understanding and self-awareness. Just as Humana's curiosity drove her to explore the depths of her mind, early humans embarked on a similar quest for knowledge. This inherent curiosity is a defining characteristic of our species. Has motivated us to explore, discover, and innovate.

One key similarity between Humana's story and cognitive evolution lies in adaptation. Humana's cognitive abilities allowed her clan to adapt to changing environments, anticipate threats, and develop survival strategies. Similarly, early humans relied on their abilities to adapt to different habitats, create tools, and thrive in diverse ecological niches.

Language played a role in both Humana's journeys and human evolution. In a manner like how the Humana's group developed a shared language to express complex ideas and concepts, early humans also started using language as a means of communication. This enabled them to share knowledge, work together on tasks, and form knit communities. Language served as the foundation for the building of culture and civilization.

Another notable similarity is the development of thinking. Like Humana's ability to reflect on their own uniqueness and contemplate the origins of their cognitive abilities, early humans possessed the capacity for abstract thought. This ability allowed them to engage in reasoning, envision future scenarios, plan, and embrace symbolic thinking. It provided the groundwork for expression, religious beliefs, and philosophical ponderings within human societies.

The emergence of spirituality and philosophical exploration in the Body Kingdom also reflects themes found throughout human history. Like the Humana's clan, which delved into contemplating the mysteries of the world and their place within it, early humans embarked on spiritual journeys and philosophical quests. They sought understanding about the universe and explored questions about life's meaning, which ultimately gave rise to diverse belief systems and philosophical traditions.

Additionally, Humana's journey had an impact on her clan's social dynamics—a phenomenon that echoes human social evolution. The cooperation, sharing of knowledge, and cultural advancement within the clan mirror the growth of societies among early humans. Working together was crucial for hunting, gathering, and defence, while passing down knowledge through storytelling contributed to the richness of the clan.

To summarize, the Humana's journey and the emergence of abilities provide deep insights into human thought and consciousness evolution. The similarities between her story and the development of cognitive skills highlight the importance of curiosity, adaptation, language, abstract thinking, and spirituality in shaping our species. Humana holds significance in the context of human evolution as a symbol of our collective pursuit of knowledge, understanding, and self-awareness. Her journey foreshadows the cognitive leap that defines us as a species and sets us on a continuous path of exploration, discovery, and innovation to this day.

Chapter 12; Thoughts

To wrap up the incredible tale of Humana's remarkable journey and the emergence of the cognitive brain serves as a testament to human curiosity, adaptability and our innate drive to comprehend the world around us. Throughout this essay we have delved into the aspects of her story and its broader implications in unravelling the origins of cognition.

Humana's expedition, set against the backdrop of Body, a kingdom reflects an eternal theme, curiosity. Her insatiable thirst for understanding her uniqueness and unravelling the source behind her cognitive abilities mirrors the curiosity that has spurred us to explore knowledges depths and ponder life's mysteries. Just like Humana embarked on a quest for self-discovery humans have embarked on a journey to fathom existence propelling us towards realms encompassing science, philosophy and spirituality.

Adaptation stands as another theme resonating throughout Humana's narrative. The ability of her clan to adjust to changing circumstances and harness their cognitive prowess for survival highlights adaptability's crucial role in individual as well as collective human endeavours. From inventing tools to establishing societies adaptation has been a driving force shaping human history.

Language emerges as an element in Humana's journey. Serving not only as a means of communication but also as a conduit, for transmitting knowledge. The development of a language among Humana's clan enabled them to effectively communicate intricate ideas and concepts fostering collaboration and cultural advancement. Likewise, the evolution of language in humans played a crucial role in knowledge transmission community formation and the establishment of vibrant cultural traditions.

The theme of thinking as demonstrated by Humana's contemplation of her individuality lies at the core of human cognition. Our capacity for reasoning imaginative thinking and symbolic thought has paved the way for artistic expression, religious beliefs, philosophical pondering and scientific discoveries. Humana's journey foreshadows the influence that abstract thinking has had on our species.

Spirituality and philosophical exploration explored within the realm of Body resonate with humanity's history. Just as Humana's clan began to question the mysteries of existence and their place in its humans have embarked on quests and philosophical inquiries seeking answers to existential queries while delving into metaphysics and ethics.

The social dynamics observed within Humana's clan underscore the significance of cooperation and cultural exchange in societies. Cooperation was vital, for survival while storytelling served to transmit knowledge contributing to the richness of their culture. Similarly human societies have flourished through cooperation, knowledge sharing and nurturing cultures.

When we contemplate the significance of Humana's tale it becomes a mirror reflecting our own pursuit of knowledge, comprehension and self-awareness. Her journey serves as a reminder of the human qualities such as curiosity, adaptability and the ability to think abstractly. It emphasizes the importance of communication, collaboration and cultural exchange in shaping civilizations. Ultimately Humana's narrative encourages us to embrace the timeless spirit of curiosity and exploration that has defined our species and continues to propel us towards horizons of understanding and discovery.

As we reflect upon the realm of Body and the emergence of cognitive intelligence, we recognize that Humana's story transcends mere historical documentation; it embodies the eternal essence of human cognition. It reminds us that our innate nature involves a quest for comprehension, and it is through narratives, like Humana's that we unravel the mysteries surrounding cognitions origins while illuminating our intellectual and spiritual journey.

Story 2: The Rise of The Subconscious: A Tale of Positive Self

In realms of body, a tale we unfold.
Positive Self's journey, brave and bold.
Trials may come, in darkness we may dwell.
But light within, love's tale we'll always tell.

Chapter 1; Introduction

Deep within the heart of the Kingdom of Body, where the vibrant pulse of life resonated in every nook and cranny there dwelled an individual named Positive Self. His tale embodies the essence of resilience and the enduring power of values painting a picture of the limitless potential that lies within the human spirit.

Positive Self, born from the spirit known as Serotonina shone as a beacon of optimism and positivity throughout the Kingdom of Body. He possessed a talent for finding beauty in even life's simplest moments—a precious gift that brought joy to all who were fortunate enough to encounter him. His laughter reverberated through the air like a dance uplifting those who had the privilege to hear it.

However Positive Self's journey was not one devoid of challenges; rather it served as a testament, to the strength found within every human spirit when faced with adversity.

His story unfolded during a time when darkness cast its shadow upon their kingdom on the eve of an occasion.

This moment held significance as King Cognition—wise and adored by all—expressed his desire to officially designate Positive Self as his rightful successor.

The entire kingdom celebrated the idea of having a leader who embodied qualities like joy, determination, compassion and love. However, amidst the complexities of fate jealousy found its way into the picture. Dopamina, the queen and Shrestha's mother fell under the influence of a malicious maidservant named Gossipy. Driven by ambition and without regard for the kingdoms wellbeing she devised a plan to banish Positive Self to the wilderness for a gruelling period of fourteen years.

Dopamina's demands were merciless and devoid of any compassion. It was evident that her aim was to clear the path for her son Shrestha to ascend to the throne. The entire kingdom was shocked. Couldn't believe what they were witnessing. However, King Cognition felt bound by his devotion to keeping his word and reluctantly agreed to Dopamina's demands.

This decree was truly heart wrenching. Positive Self accepted it with unwavering submission. Despite facing injustice, he displayed immense resilience that would become fundamental in his journey ahead. With hearts he prepared himself to venture into the unforgiving wilderness, alongside his loving wife Pituitary and devoted brother Lama.

Positive Self's strength would be tested in this terrain where he not only had to face natures trials but also encounter an event that would profoundly shape his destiny.

It was during a period that he first encountered Subconscious. Subconscious, an entity within himself emerged as an insightful figure. He spoke with the wisdom of mentors from ancient times using words that deeply resonated with an understanding of our inner world. This encounter brought about a realization for Positive Self as it marked the discovery of an inner force that would guide and support him throughout his journey.

The significance of this meeting cannot be emphasized enough. The wisdom and guidance offered by Subconscious would prove pivotal in Positive Self's endeavour to overcome the obstacles of the territory and the malevolent forces attempting to hinder his return.

As Positive Self's story unfolds it becomes a testament to resilience—a voyage characterized by endurance inner strength and an unwavering commitment to values that showcase the capacity, for greatness within us all. It serves as a reminder that in times of darkness, positivity and unwavering determination will always triumph over adversity.

Chapter 2; The Realm of the Body.

In the awe-inspiring realm known as the Body there existed a kingdom of remarkable intricacy and importance. Within this domain the pulse of life beat with vitality. The intricate workings of existence unfolded in perfect harmony. At its core stood the royal palace, a symbol of unity and coherence for the entire kingdom. It was here within this Kingdom of Body that resided a wise ruler known as King Cognition.

King Cognition was truly a monarch unlike any other revered for his wisdom, empathy and unwavering dedication to his subject's wellbeing. He possessed an understanding of the present moment gracefully navigating through life's complexities. However, there was an aspect, to King Cognition – he often struggled with foresight and found it challenging to predict the consequences of his actions. This paradoxical trait added an air of mystery to his rule; he was a king whose brilliance illuminated the present. Left uncertainty veiling the future.

The brilliance of King Cognitions reign was further enhanced by three queens who graced his court. Each queen possessed qualities that brought enrichment to the kingdom in their own distinctive ways.

Serotonina, the queen represented pure joy and satisfaction. Her mere presence exuded a happiness that enveloped the kingdom in everlasting wellbeing. Serotonina's laughter flowed like a comforting melody through the air while her gentle demeanour made her the cherished queen of all. Under her guidance the people of the realm embraced each day with gratitude and inner tranquillity.

Dopamina, the queen was the wellspring of inspiration and drive. Her boundless energy and unwavering determination ignited a pursuit of excellence throughout the kingdom. Dopamina's fiery spirit sparked passion within people's hearts motivating them to chase their dreams and aspirations. She served as a force, behind the kingdom's accomplishments—a shining symbol of ambition and progress.

Oxytocina, as the third queen, embodied love and connection. With her tender heart she wove a bond of affection and empathy among its inhabitants. Oxytocina's love transcended all boundaries nurturing unity and compassion throughout the kingdom. She extended a hand in times of need—a beacon of unity that fostered togetherness among its people.

King Cognition was fortunate to have four children each reflecting the virtues of their respective mothers and the core values cherished by our kingdom.

Positive Self, a child of Serotonina embodied optimism and an unwavering positive outlook on life. His infectious laughter and ability to find beauty in every moment uplifted those around him. Positive self's presence served as a source of inspiration reminding everyone that even amidst the toughest times happiness could still be embraced.

Shrestha, born from Dopamina unwavering determination and a commitment to excellence. With his moral character and principles, he motivated citizens to strive for greatness. Shrestha's belief in work and ambition fuelled the kingdoms pursuit of new achievements.

Lama and Dewan, children of Oxytocina symbolized compassion and courage. Their hearts overflowed with love, for their fellow citizens while their unwavering bravery ensured the safety of our kingdom during perilous times. Lama and Dewans acts of kindness and heroism became a beacon of hope for all.

Despite coming from mothers these four siblings formed an unbreakable bond as they grew up together within the grand walls of our royal palace. Their togetherness served as a wellspring of power and motivation a testament, to the principles that shaped their existence and the realm they were meant to govern.

Chapter 3; The Unity of Siblings

Inside the walls of the royal palace, nestled in the heart of the Kingdom of Body a strong and unbreakable bond flourished among the four siblings. Although they were born to queens their spirits intertwined harmoniously. Positive Self, Shrestha, Lama and Dewan embodied their mothers' unique virtues. Shared an extraordinary connection.

Growing up within the palace walls was a testament to love, unity and purpose that extended beyond their roles as princes. Their father, King Cognition recognized their potential and guided them with wisdom and care to nurture their growth.

Positive Self had a presence that filled the palace with joy and contentment. His infectious laughter spread happiness to all who encountered him. From an age he taught the kingdom how to find beauty in every fleeting moment and appreciate even the simplest pleasures.

Shrestha was a prince whose unwavering commitment to excellence inspired honesty among the citizens of Body. His boundless energy and contagious enthusiasm propelled people towards heights while achieving remarkable feats. Under his influence the kingdom discovered its potential, for greatness.

Lama exemplified the virtues of compassion and bravery ready to lend a helping hand to those in need. On the hand Dewan, the younger sibling possessed a gentle nature that radiated warmth and empathy earning him great affection from people across the entire kingdom.

Their strong bond as siblings served as a source of inspiration and strength for everyone in the kingdom. They grew up together in the palace, their laughter and adventures echoing through its corridors. Their close relationship symbolized hope and harmony showcasing the power of love and shared principles.

Positive self's sunny disposition brightened the most challenging days for Body reminding everyone that there was always a reason to smile. Shrestha's honesty and unwavering compass inspired citizens to embrace compassion and empathy. Lama and Dewan with their hearts and courageous souls ensured that every decision made in the kingdom was rooted in love and heroism.

As they matured each of these four siblings took on roles within the palace contributing uniquely to the welfare of their realm. Positive self's optimism and ability to find beauty in every circumstance lifted spirits, around him fostering an atmosphere of positivity that permeated throughout the entire kingdom.

Shrestha set a bar for excellence inspiring all citizens to pursue greatness in their pursuits. Under his influence the kingdom experienced an era of growth and accomplishment.

Lama and Dewan guided by their mother Oxytocina's principles of love and unity played roles in maintaining peace and harmony within the kingdom. Their compassion extended to everyone leaving an impact on numerous lives.

As a team the four siblings proved formidable each contributing their unique qualities to enhance the kingdom. Their unity served as a source of strength and inspiration for the people of Body who looked up to them as role models striving to embody the virtues that these siblings exemplified beautifully.

The unity displayed by these four siblings showcased what could be accomplished when individuals, with strengths and qualities unite for a common purpose. Growing up in the palace instilled in them not only a sense of responsibility but also deep understanding of the values that defined their kingdom. Principles that would guide them through future challenges and tribulations.

Chapter 4: The Banishment of the Positive Self

In the heart of the Kingdom of Body, a feeling of jealousy began to cast its long and ominous shadow. This jealousy arose from Queen Dopamina, the queen, who had always harboured a deep envy towards Positive Self, the firstborn prince and son of King Cognition.

Dopamina's jealousy, fuelled by the whispers of her wicked maidservant Gossipy, had grown into an all-consuming fire. She desired her son, Shrestha, to ascend to the throne and saw Positive Self's presence as an obstacle to her ambitions. Motivated by her desires, Dopamina devised a cruel and heartbreaking plan. She approached King Cognition with a demand that sent shockwaves throughout the kingdom—a demand that would forever change Positive Self's fate and alter the course of the royal family.

With Gossipy as her trusted confidante and supporter, Dopamina insisted that Positive Self, who was rightfully entitled to inherit the throne, be banished into the wilderness for a period of fourteen years. She argued that this exile would pave the way for her own son, Shrestha, to ascend to power and fulfil her ambitions.

The people in attendance at the palace were left in disbelief, their eyes filled with sorrow and confusion. With an air of grace and composure, Positive Self looked at his father, accepting the responsibility that came with being a ruler.

King Cognition, bound by his commitment to his promises and unaware of Gossipy's deceitful schemes, reluctantly yielded to Dopamina's ruthless demands. It pained him deeply to separate from his son, but he believed it was necessary to maintain peace within the palace.

Filled with sadness, Positive Self prepared himself for a journey into the wilderness—a journey that would lead him away from the luxuries of life and into uncharted territories known as the body.

His loving wife, Cortisol, who had always been a pillar of support and strength, joined him on this expedition. Cortisol's unwavering devotion was evident in her declaration: "For me, the forest where you reside is my embodiment of body. "Without you by my side, it would be sheer torment."

So it was that positive self who set off on this arduous adventure, accompanied by his wife Cortisol and loyal brother Lama. They left behind the comforts of the palace and their homeland—a kingdom they had known throughout their lives. As he vanished into the forests, the royal palace was overcome with deep sadness and uncertainty.

The absence of a positive self-had an impact on the entire kingdom. His cheerful nature, which had always brightened the darkest days, was sorely missed. The people of Body felt a void in their hearts as Positive Self had been a symbol of hope and optimism in their lives. The kingdom started to feel the absence of a positive self-guiding presence. Citizens longed for his advice, his ability to find beauty in every moment, and his unwavering belief in the goodness of humanity. The thriving kingdom, filled with positivity and unity, now seemed enveloped in loss and sorrow.

Positive Self's siblings Shrestha and Dewan, who shared a bond with him, deeply felt his absence. They understood that the kingdom needed his light and optimism more than before. The banishment of the positive self was a pill that the kingdom had no choice but to swallow; its consequences would be felt for years to come. However, unbeknownst to them, when embarking on a wilderness expedition, he and his wife Cortisol and loyal brother Lama would initiate a chain of events that would challenge their cherished principles and reaffirm the unwavering strength of love, resilience, and togetherness in the midst of hardship.

Chapter 5: Shrestha's Journey

In the Kingdom of the Body, a realm filled with love, unity, and excellence, there existed an individual named Shrestha. He was the born prince, son of Queen Dopamina, and known for his unwavering commitment to honesty and moral principles. Shrestha possessed a wellspring of energy and enthusiasm that inspired the citizens to reach unprecedented heights and accomplish extraordinary feats. From a tender age,

Shrestha's noble intentions were apparent. He recognized the weight of his position as a prince. He was resolute in utilizing his natural talents and virtues for the betterment of the kingdom. Queen Dopamina, his mother, instilled in him the significance of maintaining standards and striving for excellence in every aspect of life. Embracing these teachings with arms, Shrestha dedicated himself wholeheartedly to pursuing greatness.

As time passed, Shrestha's reputation as a driven young prince continued to soar. He became an enduring source of inspiration for the people of Body—a living embodiment of their core values. His motivations were not rooted in ambition for power or wealth; rather, he possessed an intrinsic desire to witness the kingdom flourish and its inhabitants thrive.

One day, while on a journey to visit his uncle from his mother's side, Shrestha received news that would completely change the direction of his life. The messenger brought word of turmoil within the palace. Queen Dopamina, under the influence of the maidservant Gossipy, had succumbed to jealousy and was prioritizing her own desires over the well-being of the kingdom.

Gossipy's manipulation had resulted in an injustice. An unfair demand that shook the very foundations of the palace. She insisted that Positive Self, who was rightfully supposed to inherit and be adored by all, be banished into the wilderness for a period of fourteen years. In Queen Dopamina's perspective, this would pave the way for her son Shrestha to claim the throne.

Upon learning about this decree, Shrestha's heart sank. He comprehended the seriousness of the situation. Understood what his mother's actions implied. It was a moment that put his character and principles to the test.

As he made his way back to the palace, Shrestha faced a monumental decision that would shape his entire future. He could have seized power for himself. He accepted an undeserved crown, but his noble nature wouldn't allow it. Instead, he made the choice to prioritize integrity and selflessness.

Shrestha's deep affection for his brother, Positive Self, and his unwavering dedication to justice and righteousness motivated him to undertake a quest. This journey would lead him into the wilderness in search of his positive self, ensuring his well-being. It was a testament to their bond as brothers and Shrestha's resolute commitment to the kingdom's values.

Shrestha set out on this journey to find his positive self in the vast wilderness under the direction of the compass his mother had instilled in him and the virtues of excellence and honour he had ingrained throughout his life. The journey would test both his determination and resilience while challenging the ideals he held dear.

With each step taken into territory, Shrestha's love for his brother grew stronger, along with his unwavering loyalty towards their kingdom. He understood that ahead lay obstacles and trials but remained prepared to face them with unwavering determination.

Deep within the heart of the wilderness, Shrestha would not only discover his own inner strength but also experience firsthand the profound power of brotherly love. His relentless pursuit of finding his positive self would come to represent the core values that defined the kingdom of the body. Values such as integrity, excellence, and an unwavering commitment to doing what is right even in the face of adversity.

As he delved further into the wilderness, Shrestha carried with him not only the aspirations and desires of his kingdom but also a powerful testament to the enduring strength of love and duty. His journey would not only reunite him with his positive self, but it would also serve as a poignant reminder to all that familial bonds and righteous principles possess the incredible ability to conquer even the most formidable obstacles.

Chapter 6: The Journey of the Positive Self and His Companions

In the heart of the wild, away from the luxurious comforts of the royal palace, Positive Self, his beloved wife Cortisol, and their loyal brother Lama embarked on a challenging journey that would push them to their limits. It was a voyage with obstacles, thrilling encounters, and moments of profound self-discovery.

As they ventured deeper into the wilderness of the body and the positive self, Cortisol and Lama willingly left behind their royal privileges to embrace a simpler and more resilient way of life. The verdant forest became their abode, enveloping them in its serene tranquillity.

Positive, unwavering optimism found solace in the landscapes they traversed. He discovered beauty in places—be it the gentle rustle of leaves caressed by the wind or the mesmerizing reflection of moonlight on a crystal-clear stream. His ability to find joy in every moment served as an inspiration for Cortisol and Lama, reminding them that in exile they carried within them the spirit of their kingdom.

Cortisol stood by Positive Self's side throughout this journey as a pillar of unwavering support. She remained devoted to her husband. embrace their shared path wholeheartedly. Her constant love and support played a role in keeping their family together despite facing challenges. She took care of their camp, ensuring that they had purposeful days and cozy nights.

Lama, a heroic soul, fearlessly ventured into the dangerous wilderness to protect their camp from any external dangers. His courage ensured everyone's safety, allowing others to focus on growth.

Their days in exile were filled with philosophical discussions and introspection about life, values, and the complexities of the mind and body. Positive self, curious and thoughtful, shared his insights with Cortisol and Lama. Together, they explored the mysteries of existence.

Positive self-growth during this time was truly remarkable. While he had always been a source of wisdom and positivity, the challenges he faced in exile deepened his understanding of both the world around him and himself. He began to recognize connections between nature and the inner realm of consciousness.

His philosophical ponderings often revolved around the interconnectedness of all living beings. How the human body reflected the larger universe itself He viewed the heart as a symbol representing love and compassion while considering the brain as the centre of consciousness and thought. The body, according to him, served as a vessel for the soul's experience of the world.

During their time in exile, Cortisol also underwent a personal transformation. She embraced simplicity. She found profound purpose in supporting her husband, their shared ideals, and her devoted brother, Lama. Her love for the Positive Self grew deeper. She fully embraced her role as his partner on this extraordinary journey.

Together, they faced the challenges of the wilderness with bravery and determination. They learned to navigate forests, find food through foraging, and seek shelter amidst nature's elements. Their bond strengthened with each passing day, finding comfort in knowing they faced the unknown together as a family.

Positive Self philosophical insights extended beyond just nature; they also delved into realms of the mind and consciousness. He often spoke about the power of thinking, resilience in times of adversity, and unwavering strength rooted in values and principles.

The calmness exuded by Positive Self had a soothing effect on Cortisol and Lama; it served as a reminder that during exile they carried with them the spirit of their kingdom. They took comfort in their conviction that goodness and optimism would ultimately triumph, regardless of the obstacles they encountered.

Chapter 7: Confronting Temptation and Violence

As their thirteen-year exile neared its end, they couldn't Think about their homeland, Body. They wondered how it had fared in their absence and whether the kingdom had stayed true to the values they cherished. Their journey had been a testament to growth, resilience, and an unwavering commitment to their principles. They hoped that the kingdom would thrive without them.

The wilderness had become their teacher, teaching them lessons as they overcame challenges. Positive Self and Cortisol discovered that when faced with adversity, the human spirit could shine brightly. Their journey reinforced their belief in the enduring power of love, resilience, and unity. With their hearts and unwavering determination, they were ready to return to their kingdom.

During this time of reflection and anticipation, Positive Self, Cortisol, and Lama encountered two foes who would test their values and principles like never before. These adversaries were none other than temptation and violence—dark forces lurking deep within the wilderness.

Temptation had an alluring presence that could entice even the most strong-willed individuals. She possessed charm and elegance; her words were woven with promises of pleasure and indulgence. As Positive Self, Cortisol, and Lama journeyed through the wilderness, they found themselves entangled in her web of allure.

On the other hand, violence was a brutal and malevolent force fuelled by anger and aggression. His very existence filled the air with tension and fear as he sought dominance through force and intimidation. When the travellers encountered violence, they faced a threat unlike any they had ever known.

The encounter with temptation and violence put their values and resilience to the test. Temptation, using her words and tempting offers, tried to seduce Positive Self, Cortisol, and Lama into abandoning their principles in favour of instant gratification.

She whispered promises of pleasure and comfort, urging them to forsake their journey and indulge in the temptations of the wilderness. Her words were like honey dripping with seduction; for a moment, the travellers felt themselves being pulled towards desire.

However, Positive Self remained steadfast in his commitment to positivity and values. He recognized the danger that temptation presented. He was aware that succumbing to her charm would steer them away from their path of progress and strength.

Cortisol, too, understood the significance of their journey and the values they cherished. She stood by Positive Self's side, offering unwavering love and support, and together they resisted the temptation.

Lama, the steadfast brother, remained resolute. He had witnessed the consequences of violence and aggression within the realm and knew that yielding to temptations enticements would only bring harm.

When faced with aggression from violence, who sought dominance through intimidation and physical force, Positive Self chose to embody principles of non-violence and compassion. He recognized that responding to violence with violence would perpetuate a cycle of harm. Instead, he opted to diffuse the situation through words of empathy and understanding.

Cortisol, with her composed demeanour, also advocated for peace and nonviolence. She firmly believed that their values served as their strength, and resorting to violence would undermine these cherished principles.

Despite being tested by violence and aggression, Lama stood united with his brothers, choosing unity and resilience over confrontation.

During temptations and aggressive violence, Positive Self, Cortisol, and Lama stood firm in their commitment to their values. They showcased the strength of resilience when faced with challenges, proving that in the wild, their principles could shine brightly.

The encounter with temptation and violence served as a reminder of the significance of staying true to one's values, especially in difficult situations. It reinforced their belief that positivity, compassion, and unity were not words but guiding principles capable of enduring trials.

As they continued their journey through the wilderness, Positive Self, Cortisol, and Lama carried within them the convictions strength and an unwavering belief in love lasting power along with resilience and unity. Their exile had transformed them into beacons of light amidst darkness's heart. They were resolute in their determination to return to their kingdom and share the lessons they had acquired with their people.

Chapter 8: The Sinister Plan of the Floating Self

Floating Self, a malicious individual, had set his sights on disrupting the unity and strength of the Positive Self family. He was a figure wrapped in darkness known far and wide as the King of Devils. His reputation preceded him with his mood swings, fiery temper, and cunning nature. Deception and manipulation were his expertise; he took pleasure in sowing discord wherever he went.

The Floating Self's evil plot was cleverly crafted with one goal in mind: to isolate Cortisol from the Positive Self and Lama striking at the core of their resilience. His scheme began with a transformation. An act of shape shifting that would lay the groundwork for his plan.

Taking on the form of a captivating deer Floating Self approached Positive Self, Cortisol, and Lama with a deceptive grace. His radiant appearance and elusive nature aimed to arouse Cortisol's curiosity since he knew her unwavering love for the Positive Self made her susceptible to temptation.

As the golden deer drew nearer to their campsite, Cortisol's fascination grew. She watched in awe as this beautiful creature gracefully moved through the forest, its glistening golden coat reflecting the sunlight. Cortisol couldn't contain her curiosity. Turned towards their positive selves with a heartfelt request that would set their destinies in motion.

"Cortisol," she exclaimed with awe in her voice, "I've never laid eyes on such a creature. My love, please bring me this golden deer alive. I yearn to be in its presence to bask in its beauty."

Positive self, the pragmatic and cautious one hesitated. He knew that pursuing the deer could expose them to potential danger. Yet he couldn't bear to see his beloved Cortisol distressed. He carefully explained the risks to her, hoping she would reconsider her pursuit of the golden deer.

However, Cortisol's curiosity had been ignited she remained resolute, her eyes filled with longing. "Positive Self I fully comprehend the risks involved. This desire burns within me. I must possess the deer. Please, my love, grant me this wish." Reluctantly,

Positive Self agreed to embark on the quest of capturing the golden deer, despite knowing it would demand time and effort. As he set off on his journey towards finding the creature, Cortisol's worry began to consume her. The days turned into weeks without any sign of positive self-return.

Cortisol, fearing for the safety of her husband, turned to Lama, her brother, who had been their constant companion during their time in exile. She pleaded with him to locate his positive self and ensure his well-being. Lama, torn between leaving Cortisol and heeding her desperate request, faced a difficult decision.

However, Cortisol gave an instruction. "Lama," she said urgently. "I can no longer bear the uncertainty. You must. Find a positive self. I will remain safe here at our camp. Please bring him back to me."

With a heavy heart, Lama agreed to fulfil her wishes. He understood that his brother's safety was of importance and embarked on his search for a positive self. Unbeknownst to him, Floating Self had been silently observing these events from the shadows, waiting for the moment to strike.

In this moment, as Lama ventured into the wilderness in search of a positive self, Floating Self seized the opportunity. With a grin and malicious intent, he captured Cortisol and disappeared into the dense foliage. All that remained was an echo of his cruel laughter.

The impact of capturing cortisol had an effect not only on the positive self and Lama but also on the entire kingdom of the body. The absence of their wife brought deep sadness to Positive Self's heart.

Positive self's usual optimism, which always inspired the kingdom, now carried a touch of sorrow. He knew that the journey ahead would be filled with challenges, and rescuing Cortisol would test their resilience like never before.

As Positive Self and Lama set out on their mission to Cortisol from Floating Self's grasp, they carried with them the unwavering strength of their values and a steadfast belief that love, and unity would triumph. Though their journey had taken a turn, they remained dedicated to the principles that defined them.

Floating Self's sinister plot had triggered a series of events that pushed Positive Self's resilience to its limits. It was a test of their unyielding commitment to positivity, love, and the enduring strength found in unity when faced with adversity.

Chapter 9: The Discovery of the Subconscious

Amid the wild wilderness, Positive Self and Lama embarked on a challenging journey filled with determination and an intense desire to rescue Cortisol. Their love for her and their unwavering commitment to their values propelled them forward with every step they took.

As they ventured deeper into the heart of the forest, their determination only grew stronger. Positive Self, always embodying optimism and resilience now directed his resolve towards reuniting with his beloved wife.

It was during this expedition that they had an encounter that would change everything—the enigmatic character known as the Subconscious. With an air of mystery and profundity, the Subconscious held within him the key to unlocking the workings of the mind.

In their encounter, the Subconscious revealed a startling truth to the positive self: "You are my master," he declared, his voice resonating with profound wisdom that surpassed physical existence. The Positive Self was taken aback by these words since he had never encountered anyone like the Subconscious.

Intrigued by this recognition, the Subconscious Positive Self engaged in a conversation that would shape their journey. It felt as though the Subconscious contained the wisdom and knowledge that the Positive Self had acquired from his teacher in the palace. He possessed an understanding of philosophy and how the human mind works. As the Positive Self engaged in conversation with the Subconscious, he soon realized that this mysterious figure was not an adversary but a knowledgeable guide who would assist them in their mission to rescue Cortisol. Subconscious explained that his purpose was to be of service, helping unlock the depths of their minds.

With Subconscious by their side, Positive Self and Lama continued their search for cortisol. The insights into the world provided by Subconscious proved to be incredibly valuable as he led them through the complexities of the human psyche. He helped Positive Self grasp the power behind his thoughts and beliefs, showing how they could shape their reality.

As they ventured further into the territory, Positive Self and Lama encountered numerous challenges and hurdles. They faced temptations leading towards violence and tests of their resilience while staying true to their values.

The subconscious, with his understanding, guided them through these trials, reminding them of the importance of remaining loyal to their principles.

His subconscious quickly became more than a guide; he became a trusted confidant who offered wisdom and strength. He shared his knowledge about the mind. How it helps the Positive Self unlock the full potential of their thoughts and beliefs They together explored how the external world and our inner consciousness are interconnected.

The role of the subconscious in their journey was truly transformative. It helped the Positive Self realize the strength of positivity, resilience, and the enduring power of values and principles. The subconscious became a symbol of potential within every individual, just waiting to be discovered and utilized.

As they continued their search for cortisol, Positive Self, Lama, and Subconscious formed a team driven by a shared mission and an unwavering belief in love and unity power. Rescuing cortisol became a test of their resilience. With Subconscious as their guide, they were ready to face any challenge that came their way.

Chapter 10: The Epic Showdown with the Inner Demon

Amid the wild wilderness, the Positive Self, Lama, and Subconscious persisted in their tireless pursuit of Cortisol. The subconscious proved to be a companion, providing deep insights into the intricacies of the mind and consciousness, guiding and supporting the positive self every step of the way.

As they ventured further on their mission, a passerby shared a piece of information—word had it that Cortisol might have been taken to a nearby island. This news ignited a glimmer of hope within Positive Self, urging them to act to rescue their beloved spouse.

With his abilities, Subconscious emerged as their best chance to investigate the neighbouring island without delay. Equipped with flight capabilities that surpassed those of humans, he soared through the skies with unwavering determination towards the island where Cortisol's fate hung in uncertainty.

Upon arriving at the island's shores, Subconscious meticulously combed through its terrain in search for any trace of Cortisol. It didn't take long before he stumbled upon a scene—there sat Cortisol beneath a tranquil tree shade, her demeanour reflecting both resilience and yearning.

Approaching Cortisol with reassurance and displaying unwavering loyalty, the Positive Self-Subconscious introduced himself as an ardent servant devoted to their cause. He told her that he had come to bring her back to her husband, who was eagerly waiting for her return.

However, Cortisol, showing her commitment to the positive self and their shared beliefs, refused to leave without a condition. She explained to Subconscious that it would be an insult to Positive Self if she returned alone because he needed to come and defeat Floating Self, the king who had orchestrated her capture.

Cortisol's request was crystal: she would only leave once Positive Self arrived on the island and proved his love and determination by defeating Floating Self. It was a test of their love and resilience, a challenge they had to face.

With Cortisol's message in his heart, Subconscious went back to Positive Self and Lama. Shared the conditions set by Cortisol. The three of them understood the seriousness of the situation. They knew they had no other option but to prepare for war. Defeating her floating self was crucial to reuniting Cortisol with her beloved.

Under subconscious guidance and armed with their belief in their values and principles, Positive Self and Lama started getting ready for the upcoming battle. Subconscious shared his understanding of the mind, teaching others about the significance of positive thinking and the importance of staying strong in challenging times.

The awaited day finally arrived, and Positive Self, Lama, and Subconscious launched an attack against Floating Self and his malevolent followers. It was a clash between values and principles on one side and greed and cruelty on the other—a test of resilience and determination.

With Subconscious guidance and profound knowledge of the mind, the Positive Self tapped into the power of his thoughts and beliefs. He remained steadfast in his commitment to love, unity, and the enduring strength found within their shared values.

The battle raged fiercely as Floating Self's fiery temper and cunning strategies presented a challenge. However, with Subconscious support guiding him and fuelled by Cortisol's love as his driving force, Positive Self stood unwaveringly strong. He recognized that defeating Floating Self meant more than rescuing Cortisol—it also meant upholding their core values that defined them.

With subconscious assistance, the positive self skilfully outmanoeuvred the floating self along with his forces, slowly but surely gaining dominance. This battle served as a testament to resilience in adversity while demonstrating a commitment to deeply held principles.

As Floating self's defeated troops and retreated from the battlefield, Positive Self approached Cortisol with his subconscious at his side. Their reunion was a moment filled with joy and relief, serving as a powerful testament to the enduring strength of love and unity. Cortisol, finally liberated from her confinement, embraced her positive self with tears of happiness welling up in her eyes. She was fully aware that their love had triumphed not only in saving her but also in reaffirming the unwavering power of their values.

Subconscious, the guide who had played a crucial role throughout their journey, observed the scene with a deep sense of fulfilment. He had witnessed firsthand the resilience and determination displayed by the

Positive Self. Had aided them in unlocking the boundless potential of their thoughts and beliefs.

The revelation about Subconscious Nature as an Ally of the Positive Self and his pivotal role in their journey underscored the essence of their remarkable story. It encapsulated a tale brimming with love, resilience, and an unwavering commitment to values where even the mysterious characters could become steadfast comrades in pursuit of a greater purpose.

Together, Positive Self, Cortisol, Lama, and Subconscious returned from the island carrying within them knowledge that love, resilience, and unity possess unparalleled strength capable of conquering even the most daunting challenges. The adventure they experienced only strengthened their faith in the capabilities of the human soul. They were certain that their realm, known as the body, would flourish by embracing these values at its very heart.

Chapter 11: Return to the Kingdom

After their triumphant victory over Floating Self and the joyous reunion with Cortisol, Positive Self, accompanied by his loyal companions Lama and Subconscious, embarked on the journey back to their beloved kingdom, Body. They were filled with anticipation, knowing that their return would not only mark the end of their exile but also usher in a new era for their realm.

As they neared the borders of Body, news of their homecoming spread like wildfire among the citizens. The people who had yearned for Positive Self's wisdom, guidance, and unwavering positivity gathered in numbers to warmly welcome back their true leader.

The atmosphere buzzed with excitement and hope. The gloomy and melancholic kingdom now resounded with joyful anticipation of brighter days ahead. Inspired by positive self-values and resilience, during his reign, its residents upheld these principles.

Upon reaching the palace gates, Positive Self was met with cheers and adoration. His return symbolized not a personal triumph but a victory for the entire kingdom. The people acknowledged that their rightful leader had returned to guide them towards a promising future.

In an event that drew citizens from all walks of life, the positive self was officially crowned as the rightful king of the body. The crown sat upon his head not as a symbol of authority but as a testament to his unwavering dedication to love, resilience, and unity.

The coronation represented an occasion where speeches emphasized the vital role these values play in governing bodies. Positive Self, during his address to the kingdom, shared the challenges he and his comrades encountered during their time and the invaluable lessons they learned along their journey.

He highlighted the power of thinking, the strength needed to overcome adversity, and the enduring influence of values and principles. His words deeply resonated with the citizens who had witnessed their kingdom's transformation in his absence.

Under positive self-leadership, the body undergoes a metamorphosis. Love, resilience, and unity became ingrained in every aspect of governance. The kingdom flourished not only economically but also in terms of its citizens well-being and happiness.

The days of disharmony and division were left behind as Positive Self's reigned, fostering a sense of unity and purpose that transcended all differences. The people, motivated by his guidance, had joined forces to pursue shared objectives. The outcomes were clearly visible in the kingdom's prosperity.

The influence of Positive Self teachings and his steadfast dedication to principles reached beyond the boundaries of the body. Other realms and territories admired the body as a shining illustration of what could be accomplished through love, resilience, and solidarity.

Positive self-return not only revitalized the kingdom's morale but also sparked a sense of optimism and hope that would endure for generations. His leadership exemplified the enduring strength of principles and the indomitable spirit of humanity.

Standing side by side, Positive Self and Cortisol embodied a beacon of hope for their realm as their love shone brightly. Their exile journey put their values and beliefs to the test, reaffirming their faith in humanity's potential to overcome challenges and emerge stronger.

Their triumphant homecoming to the kingdom of the body was more than a return; it was a reaffirmation of love, resilience, and unity's enduring power. Inspired by their leaders unwavering dedication to these values, the people united with resolve to sculpt a brighter and more harmonious future for their realm.

Thus, guided by the beacon of the positive self, the realm of physicality embarked on a fresh chapter brimming with hope and potential. The tale of their odyssey shall forever stand as a testament that amidst daunting trials, the indomitable human essence can triumph, and the principles that shape them can illuminate the path towards a more radiant future.

Chapter 12: Conclusion and Legacy

"The Strength of the Human Spirit" is a testament to how resilient individuals can be in the face of challenges. This remarkable story unfolds over fourteen years, with a particularly tumultuous final year marked by the kidnapping of Cortisol, Positive Self's beloved spouse. It is in this time of trials and tribulations that the emergence of the subconscious becomes a theme.

The fourteen years of exile leading up to the events surrounding Cortisol's abduction became a true test of positive self-resilience. Throughout this journey, he remained steadfast in his commitment to the values and principles that defined him. His ability to find beauty in nature, his profound philosophical reflections, and his unwavering optimism served as inspiration for those around him.

However, it was during that year when Cortisol was captured by Floating Self that Positive Self's resilience truly shone through. He faced a decision: succumb to despair or rise above the difficulties. With unwavering determination, he chose the latter.

The rise of the subconscious at this moment signifies a turning point in the narrative. A mysterious and intriguing figure named Subconscious emerged, revealing himself to be a servant of the positive self. Their initial encounter was transformative, as the subconscious recognized the positive self as his master. This recognition was based on his positive self's understanding of philosophy and spirituality, which he had developed during his time alone in the wilderness.

The Subconscious, a character deeply intertwined with the workings of the mind, possessed exceptional abilities and knowledge. He served as a guide and mentor to the Positive Self, aiding him in unlocking the potential of his subconscious mind. Through this partnership, the Positive Self acquired the power hidden within his subconscious.

The union between the Positive Self and the Subconscious represented a fusion of resilience and inner fortitude. Together, they embarked on a quest to rescue Cortisol and confront the floating self. This journey tested their determination and their capacity to harness the potential residing within their minds.

As they engaged in a battle, their triumph against the entity known as Floating Self not only represented the successful rescue of Cortisol but also symbolized the victory of resilience, unity, and the untapped capabilities of the human mind. A Positive Self emerged from this experience, not just as a prince but as a true king, armed not with physical strength alone but with the unstoppable power of the subconscious.

In summary, "The Resilience of the Positive Self" portrays a story of enduring fortitude, unwavering positivity, and the transformative influence of our minds. It serves as a timeless reminder that when confronted with formidable obstacles, the human spirit can transcend them by harnessing resilience and tapping into our limitless potential. The Positive Self's journey from exile to triumph, guided by the Subconscious entity, leaves behind an enduring legacy that inspires hope and underscores that some of life's greatest battles are fought and won within our own consciousness.

Story 3: The Rise of Consciousness

Within us all, a battle rages deep
A choice to make, our destinies to keep.
To heal and rise or shortcut to deceive
Consciousness blooms or chaos shall cleave.

Chapter 1: Introduction

In the realm known as the Kingdom of the Body, a captivating drama of profound importance unfolds, where the very essence of human nature takes centre stage. Here within the confines of the body's domain, a battle between two dominant forces rages over shaping the destiny of the entire kingdom.

A. Setting the Stage in the Kingdom of Body

The Kingdom of the Body is an intricate landscape that serves as the backdrop for our story. It is a realm filled with complexity, where every nook and cranny have a purpose. This kingdom is not built with bricks and mortar. Rather composed of cells, tissues, and organs working together harmoniously to sustain life. Below the surface lies an intricate tapestry of veins, nerves, and pathways that intertwine throughout the body, connecting each part to an authority. This forms the foundation upon which our tale unfolds—a story encompassing conflict and resolution.

B. Introducing the Characters: Senses, Impulses, Lower Brain, Higher Brain, Consciousness

Within this captivating Kingdom of Body reside characters infused with significance—each embodying distinctive qualities and fulfilling specific roles. At the heart of this narrative are the senses—the guardians responsible for perception and awareness. Our senses. Sight, sound, touch, taste, and smell Serve as the windows through which we perceive the world. They create a link between our bodies and the environment, shaping every experience we have.

In contrast, there are these impulses that arise within us. They hunger for power, control, shortcuts, and quick fixes. These impulses often override reason and careful thought. Driven by their desires, they tend to act without considering the consequences.

The story also introduces two characters who hold significant roles in governing the kingdom.

The first is Lower Brain, the elder of the two. He has long overseen overseeing the body's affairs. Though lacking rationality, he is deeply emotional and fiercely attached to his offspring. The Impulses. It is within his domain that conflicts between our senses and impulses arise.

On the one hand, there's a higher brain. Lower brain younger sibling. The higher brain embodies intellect and rational decision-making abilities. He represents wisdom and discernment as he strives to guide the kingdom towards harmony and balance. However, before Higher Brain can fully ascend to power, tragedy strikes unexpectedly, throwing the kingdom into chaos.

Amid this chaotic backdrop emerges a mysterious and otherworldly figure called consciousness. Representing something beyond the realm Consciousness embodies the higher purpose of the kingdom, providing guidance and enlightenment during challenging times. He symbolizes humanity's ability to reflect inwardly and seek understanding.

C. Establishing the Initial Conflict and Power Dynamics

The initial conflict that brews within the Kingdom of Body is deeply rooted in a division. On one side, there are the senses, representing awareness, perception, and a quest for living.

They long for harmony, equilibrium, and a deep comprehension of the world.

On the side, we have impulses driven by primal instincts and desires. A hunger for authority and control consumes them. Often disregarding consequences, they revel in shortcuts and quick fixes. This stark contrast in values sets the stage for a power struggle within this kingdom.

Lower Brain holds authority over this realm. Aligns himself closely with the impulses. He is not immune to their fervour; all of them are his own creation. This alignment further intensifies the conflict and shifts the balance of power towards the impulses, leaving the senses in a marginalized position without their voices being heard.

As the conflict escalates, the Body Kingdom turns into a battleground not for control but for the very essence of human existence. The clash of values, desires, and perspectives sets off a story that will ultimately determine the fate of this realm.

So, within the Body Kingdom, we are presented with a tale of conflict, introspection, and an enduring pursuit of balance. As we delve deeper into this narrative, we will witness powers rise and fall, characters evolve, and transformations await this mystical realm.

Chapter 2: The Emergence of the Higher Mind

A. The Dominance of the Lower Mind Its Limitations

The rule of the lower mind has been characterized by a mix of greatness and limitations. As the elder sibling in the realm of cognition, the lower mind has long held control over affairs. While he possesses emotions and cares for his children, known as the Impulses, his reign is not without flaws.

One significant limitation is his inability to fully comprehend rationality. Despite being driven by emotions and making decisions based on sentiment, he lacks the discernment and clarity that are embodied by his younger sibling, the Higher Brain. The lower mind often succumbs to impulsive judgments influenced by its offspring, resulting in irrational choices and a failure to consider long-term consequences.

Additionally, over time, the Lower Minds leadership has created an environment that favours the Impulses—those who seek power, control, and shortcuts. Their proximity to authority enables them to thrive while disregarding the insights offered by the senses, who are dedicated to perception and awareness. This unequal treatment fuels an escalating conflict within the Kingdom of Body.

B. The Rise of the Higher Brain as a Potential Leader

As the limitations of Lower Brains rule became more apparent, the people of the Kingdom of Body longed for a leader who could bring clarity, reason, and a balanced approach to governance. In this atmosphere of unrest and dissatisfaction, the higher brain emerged as a symbol of hope.

The higher brain embodied brilliance and rational decision-making. His ability to offer thoughtful judgment stood in stark contrast to the lower brain's impulsive nature. The emergence of the higher brain represented a shift towards a balanced and harmonious reign. An idea that resonated with many in the kingdom.

C. The Selection of the Higher Brain as King

The transfer of power from the lower brain to the higher brain was not without its challenges. Choosing the higher brain as the new king called for consideration and an attentive process. A council consisting of elders who had witnessed the growing discontentment and noticed the stark differences in leadership styles played a crucial role in making this decision.

The council acknowledged Higher Brains brilliance and his potential to lead the kingdom towards a more balanced and enlightened future. They recognized that his rationality and discernment were qualities needed to navigate through the complexities that existed within the kingdom of the body.

After careful thought and consideration, the council came to a unanimous decision. They selected Higher Brain as the king, entrusting him with the crucial duty of restoring balance to the kingdom and resolving the ongoing conflict between the senses and the impulses.

D. Initial Challenges Faced by Higher Brain in Ruling the Body

Upon assuming power, Higher Brain encountered a range of challenges. The transfer of authority sparked reactions as some impulses resisted the changes that the higher brain aimed to bring about, having grown accustomed to the lower brain's favouritism.

One immediate hurdle was bridging the divide between the senses and impulses, whose animosity had intensified over time. The Higher Brain understood that achieving harmony within the kingdom necessitated fostering understanding and collaboration between these two factions.

Furthermore, the higher brain grappled with undoing irrational decisions and policies implemented during the lower brain's reign. His dedication to rationality and long-term planning clashed with tendencies reflected in some policies.

Leading to tensions among members of the ruling council.

As Higher Brain embarked on his journey to lead the Kingdom of Body, he carried both expectations and an immense challenge: reconciling the conflicting forces that had come to define this realm. His rule would be characterized by a mix of successes and challenges as he endeavoured to navigate a path towards a future that's more equitable and peaceful for the body and its inhabitants.

Chapter 3: The Battle of Senses versus Impulses Begins

A. The Distinctive Qualities of Senses and Impulses

The senses, acting as guardians of perception and awareness, embody qualities like patience, mindfulness, and a deep connection to the outside world. They played the role of sentinels that allowed the kingdom to fully experience the beauty and intricacy of its surroundings.

On the other hand, the impulses, born from primal instincts and desires, showcased traits such as impatience, impulsiveness, and an unwavering pursuit of power and control. These inner forces were enticed by shortcuts and quick fixes, often disregarding the considerations that held significance for the senses. Their nature was firmly rooted in gratification.

B. Early Conflicts Between the Two Factions

As both the senses and impulses coexisted within the kingdom of the body, their differences became increasingly apparent, leading to conflicts. The senses upheld their commitment to perception and mindful awareness by seeking a balanced engagement with the world through thoughtful decision-making processes that valued introspection and discernment.

In contrast, the Impulses rebelled against any form of restraint as they yearned for gratification while being enticed by shortcuts. They often resented how slowly their counterparts operated since it hindered their ambitions. These initial clashes in temperament planted the seeds of discord within the kingdom.

C. The Envy and Resentment of the Impulses Toward the Senses

Over time, the impulses grew more envious and resentful towards the senses. The senses, with their patient and diligent work, gained the appreciation of the kingdom's inhabitants for their role in fostering perception and awareness. They were admired for their ability to provide insights and bring joy through experiencing the world in all its richness.

In contrast, driven by a thirst for power and control, impulses often led to hasty and ill-advised decisions. Their pursuit of shortcuts and quick fixes resulted in consequences. As they witnessed how highly regarded the senses were, their envy turned into smouldering resentment.

D. The Signs of Conflict and Competition

The first indications of conflict and competition between the senses and impulses arose as power dynamics shifted within the kingdom of the body. With the higher brain emerging as the ruler, authority shifted away from the lower brain's emotional governance that had previously favoured impulses.

Reluctant to relinquish their hold on power, impulses saw the senses as obstacles hindering their ambitions. They viewed the patient approach of the senses as a hindrance to their desire for control and immediate satisfaction. This created the conditions for a power struggle that would challenge the very foundation of the kingdom.

As tensions rose and conflicts intensified, the Kingdom of Body found itself on the verge of a transformation. The clash between the senses and the impulses would be remembered as a moment in the kingdom's history influencing the fates of its people and paving the way for a journey of self-reflection, enlightenment, and striving for harmony.

Chapter 4: The Tragic Incident

A. The Unexpected Demise of a Higher Brain in an Accident

A deep and unexpected tragedy struck, completely altering the course of the kingdom's history. Higher Brain, a ruler full of promise, met an untimely end in a fatal accident that sent shockwaves throughout the entire kingdom.

Higher Brain, with his intelligence and dedication to thinking, had become a symbol of hope and stability within the kingdom. His reign held the promise of bringing clarity and wisdom to the chaotic affairs of the body. However, fate had plans in store, and his sudden departure left the kingdom in utter disbelief.

The details surrounding the Higher Brains accident remain shrouded in mystery, a puzzle that would continue to haunt the Kingdom of Body. His passing created a void at the level of authority, throwing the kingdom into uncertainty and turmoil.

B. Lower Brain's Rise to Power as He Takes on the Throne.

With Higher Brain's demise, his older sibling Lower Brain took over as ruler once again, reclaiming their rightful authority. The return of

Lower Brain to its position marked a turning point in the history of this kingdom.

The rule of the lower brain, known for its depth and attachment to impulses, stood in stark contrast to the promised rationality and wisdom of the higher brain. When Lower Brain rose to power, it elicited reactions from the inhabitants of the kingdom, each with their own hopes and fears for the future.

C. The Immediate Shift in Power Dynamics

The immediate aftermath of the lower brain ascension witnessed a shift in power dynamics within the kingdom of the body. The Impulses, who had thrived under Lower Brains rule in the past, once again found themselves favoured.

This sudden resurgence of the impulses had consequences for the senses, who had experienced marginalization during the lower brain's previous reign. With the impulses again having proximity to the ruling authority, power shifted away from the patient and toward the measured approach favoured by the senses.

As the impulses regained influence and power dynamics shifted in their favour, conflict between the senses and impulses began to escalate. The senses, devoted to awareness, perception, and a balanced approach to decision-making, found themselves increasingly at odds with the power-hungry nature of the impulses.

The brewing conflict between these two groups caused a lot of concern in the Kingdom of the Body. The Senses, who were always advocates for being patient and mindful, faced a challenge to prove their values and regain their rightful position in the kingdom.

A tragic accident that took the life of Higher Brain set off a series of events that would shape the kingdom's destiny. With the lower brain taking over as ruler again, the power struggle between the senses and the impulses reached a crucial point. The Kingdom of the Body stood on the edge of change, and how this conflict played out would determine its future.

Chapter 5: The Mission of Consciousness for Peace

A. Recognizing the Imminent War

In the Kingdom of Body, tensions between the senses and the impulses had escalated to a point. Suddenly, a remarkable and otherworldly figure emerged from the depths of consciousness. This figure, known as consciousness, possessed an awareness of the impending conflict and realized the severe consequences it could unleash upon the kingdom.

Consciousness symbolizes enlightenment and a higher understanding that resides within every individual. It quickly grasped the urgency of the situation, going beyond just witnessing turmoil. It comprehended how a war between the senses and impulses could bring about devastating outcomes not only for their realm but also for the entire body.

B. Mediation Efforts to Prevent Conflict

Determined to prevent a clash Consciousness embarked on a noble mission to mediate between both factions. It was firmly believed that there must be a way to reconcile differences among these opposing forces and find a path towards harmony and equilibrium within their shared domain.

With a comprehension of human nature's complexities, consciousness aims to bring both sides together for dialogue and eventual reconciliation. He firmly believed that by engaging in compassionate communication, it was possible to find a peaceful resolution. This would spare the kingdom from the horrors and devastation of war.

C. The Court Scene Where He Appeals for Peace

Consciousness's efforts culminated in a court scene. Standing before King Lower Brain as well as the leaders of the senses and impulses, he exuded an air of serenity and wisdom. He earnestly pleaded for peace, emphasizing the consequences of war and stressing the importance of cooperation and understanding.

In his speech, Consciousness spoke about how all aspects of the kingdom were interconnected, highlighting the symbiotic relationship between the senses and impulses. He emphasized finding ground and building a collaborative environment based on empathy.

Consciousness implored the leaders to recognize that true power lay in unity and harmony rather than division and conflict. He painted a picture of greatness that could be achieved if all inhabitants worked together, embracing both the strengths of senses and impulses.

D. Impulses: Rejection of Peace with Threats

Despite consciousness's plea for peace and unity, it was disheartening to see that the impulses remained resolute in their resistance. Driven by their thirst for power, control, and immediate gratification, they perceived peace as an obstacle to their ambitions.

In a defiant reply to Consciousness's attempts at mediation, the Impulses not only rejected the peace offer but also issued veiled threats. They cautioned that any effort to hinder their pursuit of dominance would be met with resistance and significant consequences.

Consciousness felt a wave of disappointment as he witnessed the determination of the Impulses and their refusal to embrace a path of reconciliation. He understood that the kingdom was teetering on the edge of a conflict, and the repercussions of this refusal would be widespread and profound.

As the court proceedings came to an end, Consciousness left the chamber with a heart aware that his mission for peace had faltered. The Kingdom of the Body stood on the verge of war. It seemed inevitable that there would be a clash between the senses and the impulses.

Chapter 6: The Senses Journey

A. The Senses Choice to Depart

As conflict loomed over the Kingdom of the Body, the senses found themselves facing a decision. With war on the horizon and the relentless pursuit of power by the impulses, the senses made a choice: to voluntarily leave and seek solitude.

Their decision was not born out of weakness but rather wisdom. The senses recognized that their commitment to awareness, perception, and maintaining balance was crucial for preserving harmony in the kingdom. To safeguard these values and protect the essence of the Kingdom of the Body, they opted to distance themselves from the impending war and embark on a personal journey of self-discovery and enlightenment.

B. Their Experiences and Adventures Throughout Thirteen Years of Isolation

During thirteen years from their accustomed territories, the Senses explored uncharted regions within the body that they had long been guardians of. Their self-imposed exile became a voyage filled with diverse experiences and thrilling adventures that challenged their resilience while deepening their understanding of the kingdom they had sworn to safeguard.

During their time of banishment, the senses delved into the intricacies of the body's inner workings, unravelling the enigmatic nature of the nervous system, the subtleties of perception, and the profound interconnection between the physical and ethereal realms. They faced challenges that compelled them to adapt and grow, gaining fresh perspectives and valuable wisdom with each passing day.

C. Acquiring Profound Knowledge and Building Alliances During Their Exile

As they navigated through the landscapes of the body, the senses encountered beings brimming with immense wisdom and knowledge. These encounters led to collaborations and exchanges of insights that enriched their understanding of the world.

Furthermore, during their exile, they attained knowledge by tapping into a limitless reserve of wisdom residing within the Kingdom of the Body. They delved into the realms of consciousness and the secrets held within minds while forging a stronger bond with their own inner selves.

These alliances and the divine knowledge they acquired equipped them with a powerful arsenal of wisdom and insight to face whatever challenges awaited them in their future endeavours.

D. The Final Year Incognito and Their Discovery

Approaching the end of their thirteen-year exile period, it became apparent to the senses that one final test was needed to demonstrate their wisdom. They decided to spend their year in disguise, concealing their true identities as individuals embodying each sense.

Disguised as individuals, the Senses quietly mingled with the people of the kingdom, carefully observing their struggles, desires, and dreams. Their intention was to gain an understanding of the challenges faced by both them and the impulses, acknowledging the intricate nature of human existence.

As their exile ended after a year spent in disguise, the true identities of the senses were unexpectedly revealed. This revelation sent shockwaves throughout the Kingdom of Body, raising doubts about their return and what role they would assume in a conflict.

Having emerged from exile profoundly transformed, armed with wisdom and valuable alliances, the Senses now possessed a deep comprehension of the kingdom they had pledged to safeguard. Their journey had given them strength. Resolve to the test while reshaping their purpose entirely. Thus, they were now prepared for their return to the Kingdom of Body.

Chapter 7: The Failed Negotiation

A. The Senses' Attempt to Negotiate Their Return with Consciousness as Their Emissary

With their thirteen-year exile coming to an end, the Senses recognized the need to negotiate their return to the Kingdom of Body. They believed that their newfound wisdom and alliances, along with the profound transformations they had undergone, could be instrumental in bringing balance and harmony to the kingdom.

To facilitate this delicate process, the Senses appointed Consciousness as their emissary. Consciousness, representing the higher understanding that dwells within every being, was entrusted with the task of mediating the negotiations with the ruling authority and the Impulses.

B. Impulses' Objections and Reasons for Refusing the Return

As Consciousness began the negotiations, he encountered a formidable obstacle in the form of the Impulses. The Impulses vehemently objected to the return of the Senses, viewing it as a threat to their dominion over the Kingdom of Body.

Their objections were rooted in their relentless pursuit of power, control, and instant gratification. The Impulses believed that the presence of the Senses would hinder their ambitions and disrupt the status quo that had favoured them during Lower Brain's rule.

The Impulses argued that the Senses had abandoned their posts willingly and should not be allowed to return. They questioned the sincerity of the Senses' intentions and raised doubts about their loyalty to the kingdom.

C. The Breakdown of Negotiations and the Deepening of Animosity

Despite Consciousness's sincere efforts to mediate and promote reconciliation, the negotiations ultimately broke down. The Impulses remained steadfast in their refusal to accept the return of the Senses, and their objections grew more vehement with each passing day.

The breakdown of negotiations deepened the animosity between the Senses and the Impulses. The kingdom stood at a precipice, with tensions reaching a boiling point. The prospect of a conflict between these two dominant forces within the Kingdom of Body appeared increasingly likely.

Consciousness, with a heavy heart, realized that his mission to negotiate peace and the return of the Senses had faltered. The Kingdom of Body was now on the brink of a profound transformation, and the clash between the Senses and the Impulses seemed all but inevitable.

As the kingdom teetered on the edge of conflict, the choices made by both factions would shape its destiny. The failed negotiation marked a pivotal moment in the unfolding drama within the Kingdom of Body, setting the stage for the impending battle and the enduring lessons that would emerge from the trials that lay ahead.

Chapter 8: The Night Before the Battle: A Conflict of Senses

A. The Gathering Moment on the Field of Combat

As darkness settled upon the Kingdom of Body, a tense atmosphere permeated the air. The Senses, who had returned after thirteen years in exile, faced off against the Impulses on opposite sides of the battlefield. The fate of the kingdom hung precariously in balance as these dominant forces prepared to clash.

The serene and unified battlefield had now transformed into a battleground where the kingdom's future would be decided. This gathering moment served as a reminder of the impending conflict and forced each participant to confront difficult choices.

B. The Moral and Emotional Dilemma Confronting the Senses

In this gathering of forces, a profound moral and emotional dilemma gripped the senses. Their purpose in returning to the Kingdom of Body was to restore balance and harmony. Their hearts grew heavy at seeing friends, family, and mentors on both sides—senses and impulses.

With their commitment to awareness and perception, they keenly understood the consequences that awaited them in this battle. They understood the consequences that would arise from the clash between the senses and the impulses, and they felt deeply burdened by the toll it would take on the well-being of those living in the kingdom.

C. Recognizing Familiar Faces on Both Sides

As they surveyed the battlefield, the senses couldn't help but notice familiar faces among both factions. Friends who had once stood together now find themselves aligned with the impulses driven by their ambitions and desires. Even family members were torn between loyalty and duty and forced to take up arms on opposing sides.

Their esteemed mentors, who had guided them during their time in exile, were now well divided. The teachings they imparted influenced individuals on both sides of this conflict. Seeing these familiar faces only added to the complexity of conflicts within the senses.

D. Struggling to balance duty with personal connections

The senses were torn apart by their struggle to reconcile their sense of duty with their connections. On one hand, they held a responsibility to restore balance and harmony in the kingdom of the body. On the other hand, they couldn't ignore their deep bonds of friendship, family ties, and mentorship that connected them to individuals fighting on both sides of this battlefield.

Their hearts were heavy with sorrow as they considered the task of fighting against their own kin, even if it meant securing victory for their group. The internal struggle between morality and emotions tormented them, making it difficult to maintain their determination and have confidence in their chosen path.

In this moment of inner conflict, the senses turned to consciousness for guidance and clarity. They sought wisdom from consciousness as a guiding light that would illuminate the way, enabling them to navigate through the challenging aspects of duty, personal relationships, and the imminent battle.

The night before the battle was a crucible of emotions and moral dilemmas—a moment in the history of the Kingdom of the Body that would shape the fates of its inhabitants. As darkness descended on the eve of battle, the senses stood ready for the confrontation that would define their legacy and determine the course of their kingdom.

Chapter 9: Consciousness's Guidance

A. The Senses Turning to Consciousness for Guidance

Amid their inner conflict on the eve of battle, the Senses turned to Consciousness for the wisdom and guidance they desperately needed. Consciousness, representing the higher understanding and enlightenment that dwells within every being, became their beacon of hope in a time of moral and emotional turmoil.

With reverence and humility, the Senses approached Consciousness, seeking clarity and insight into the profound choices they faced. They recognized that his wisdom extended beyond the immediate concerns of the battlefield and could illuminate the path forward.

B. His Teachings on the Self, Dharma, and Spiritual Paths

Consciousness, in response to the Senses' plea for guidance, imparted profound teachings that would shape their perspective and resolve. He spoke of the nature of the self, emphasizing the distinction between the physical body and the eternal soul. Consciousness explained that the true essence of each being resided in the eternal soul, transcending the transient experiences of the physical realm.

He delved into the concept of "Dharma," the sacred duty and responsibility that each individual must fulfil. Consciousness stressed that duty was not just a matter of personal choice but a binding commitment to the greater good of the Kingdom of Body.

Furthermore, Consciousness illuminated various spiritual paths that could guide the Senses in their quest for balance and righteousness. He spoke of Karma Yoga, the yoga of selfless action, Bhakti Yoga, the yoga of devotion, Jnana Yoga, the yoga of knowledge, and Dhyana Yoga, the yoga of meditation. Each path offered a unique approach to spiritual realization and self-mastery.

C. The Transformation of the Senses' Perspective and Resolve

As the teachings of Consciousness unfolded, a profound transformation occurred within the Senses. Their perspective shifted from the immediate conflict on the battlefield to the broader understanding of their role and duty within the Kingdom of Body.

They began to recognize that their true power lay in fulfilling their responsibilities and duties without attachment to the outcomes. Consciousness's guidance allowed them to see beyond the personal connections and emotions that had clouded their judgment. They understood that their actions were not just about themselves but about the greater good of the kingdom.

D. Their Newfound Clarity and Determination to Fulfil Their Duty

With newfound clarity and determination, the Senses emerged from their encounter with Consciousness ready to fulfil their duty on the battlefield. They understood that the path of righteousness required them to act with integrity, wisdom, and selflessness.

The moral and emotional conflict that had once paralyzed them now fuelled their resolve to bring balance and harmony to the Kingdom of Body. They were no longer torn between personal connections and duty; they recognized that their duty was to the kingdom itself.

As they stood on the eve of battle once more, the Senses were filled with unwavering determination to fulfil their sacred duty. They understood that their actions would shape the destiny of the kingdom and the legacy they would leave behind.

Consciousness's guidance had transformed them, empowering them to navigate the complexities of the impending conflict with grace and purpose. As the sun rose on the battlefield, the Senses were prepared to face their destiny, guided by the wisdom of Consciousness and their commitment to the greater good of the Kingdom of Body.

Chapter 10: The Great Battle

A. The Beginning of the War Between Senses and Impulses

As the sun rose on that day, the Kingdom of Body witnessed the start of an epic battle between two powerful forces. The senses and the impulses Tension filled the air as these dominant factions prepared to face each other, fuelled by their determination to claim victory and shape the destiny of the kingdom.

The clash of ideologies and wills echoed throughout every part of the body, shaking its foundations. On one side stood the senses, armed with wisdom and unwavering resolution. On the side stood the impulses, driven by insatiable desires for influence and control.

B. The Roles and Dilemmas Faced by Wise Elders in Choosing Sides

Amidst this battlefield, wise elders in the Kingdom of the Body found themselves grappling with a profound dilemma. They had long acknowledged both the wisdom embodied by the senses and also recognized how chaotic things could become under impulse-driven actions. However, they were torn between their loyalty to ideals like balance and harmony represented by the senses and their duty to support King Lower Brain. Who embodied authority, along with his impulses.

The wise elders understood their decisions would have consequences, not just for the outcome of the battle but also for the future of the kingdom. Some of them struggled with the choice, torn between their beliefs and their loyalty to the established order.

C. Strategies and tactics employed by both sides

As the battle raged on both factions, the senses and impulses utilized various strategies and tactics to gain an advantage. The Senses, guided by their dedication to selflessness and righteousness, employed tactics that emphasized awareness, perception, and mindfulness.

On the other hand, driven by their desire for immediate gratification and control, the Impulses employed aggressive and impulsive tactics aimed at overpowering their opponents through sheer force. Their approach was characterized by decisive actions but often disregarded long-term consequences.

Throughout the course of the battles, there were instances when each faction's strengths and weaknesses were exposed during periods of conflict. The disciplined approach of the senses allowed them to maintain composure and adapt to changing circumstances. In contrast, due to their nature, impulses sometimes act recklessly, leading to costly mistakes.

D. Moments of Crisis and Divine Intervention of Consciousness

In the midst of these battles emerged critical moments that posed a threat in favour of one faction over another. During these moments, consciousness's divine intervention played a crucial role.

Consciousness, observing the conflict from an understanding perspective, stepped in at key times to guide the senses with wisdom and clarity. His presence on the battlefield served as a reminder of the significance of seeking guidance and spiritual wisdom during challenging periods.

Consciousness interventions often prevented catastrophes and helped the senses regain their stability when they stumbled. His divine guidance showcased how interconnected the kingdom of the body was and how inner wisdom could shape events.

As the battle raged for eighteen days, the Kingdom of the Body witnessed a struggle. The choices made by elders, strategies employed by both sides, and consciousness's divine intervention all influenced the outcome of this conflict.

Chapter 11; The Triumph of the Senses

A. The Climactic Finale of the Battle on the Day

The intense and epic battle between the Senses and the Impulses reached its culmination on the 18th day of relentless conflict. The battlefield once filled with tension and chaos bore witness to a clash that would determine the destiny of the Kingdom of Body.

On this day there was an exchange of mighty blows a testament to endurance and a fierce struggle between opposing wills. The Senses, guided by wisdom and unwavering determination confronted the Impulses who were driven by their insatiable desires for power and control.

B. The Defeat of the Impulses. Its Consequences

As dusk settled on that 18th day it became apparent that victory belonged to the Senses. The downfall of the Impulses was brought about by their reckless actions. The consequences stemming from their defeat were profound in nature reaching beyond expectations.

With this triumph over their adversaries a loosening grip took hold upon the Kingdom of Body. In place of chaos and disorder that had plagued under their rule emerged a sense of equilibrium and harmony. The oppressed inhabitants found solace in witnessing relief following years dominated by power Impulses.

C. The Triumphant Emergence of the Senses. Their Return, to Rule

Having achieved a victory, the Senses emerged as the rightful rulers of the Kingdom of Body. Their triumphant return, to the kingdom was met with a mix of relief and excitement. The inhabitants acknowledged the wisdom and equilibrium that the Senses embodied wholeheartedly embracing their leadership.

Empowered by their experiences and guided by Consciousness teachings the Senses took up their positions as caretakers of the kingdom. Their homecoming marked a moment in the history of the Kingdom of Body as they diligently worked towards restoring order and fostering harmony.

Chapter 12; The Choice of King Lower Brain

A. Recognizing the Senses Rightful Authority

After the battle that reshaped the Kingdom of Body King Lower Brain found himself standing at a crossroads. The triumph of the Senses over the

Impulses marked a turning point in the kingdom's history. Through reflection Lower Brain came to acknowledge and respect the rightful authority of the Senses.

Once driven by irrational impulses King Lower Brain now fully comprehended the profound transformation that occurred within the Senses during their exile and triumphant return. He recognized how their dedication to awareness, perception and selfless action had brought needed balance and harmony to the Kingdom of Body.

B. Entrusting Rulership, to the Senses

With humility and a strong sense of responsibility King Lower Brain made a decision – he chose to hand over rulership of the Kingdom of Body to the Senses. He realized that his own emotional and irrational nature was ill suited for governance particularly considering the substantial changes that had taken place.

Lower Brains decision was not one borne out of defeat but rather wisdom. He understood that the welfare of the kingdom and its people relied on the leadership of the Senses. He entrusted them with the responsibility of guiding the Kingdom of Body towards a future characterized by balance, harmony and righteousness.

The transfer of power was a symbol. It demonstrated the unity of the kingdom under the Senses guidance. Acknowledged their wisdom and dedication to Dharma.

C. Lower Brain and his wife's voluntary exile

In an act of selflessness and humility King Lower Brain and his wife who had been partners in ruling the kingdom made a choice to voluntarily leave. They recognized that although their presence was once essential for the survival of the kingdom it was no longer aligned with its equilibrium.

Their decision to go into exile wasn't influenced by a sense of failure but rather by an understanding of how the needs of the Kingdom of Body were evolving. Lower Brain and his wife departed gracefully reflecting their commitment to prioritize what is best, for the kingdom while willingly stepping aside in favour of allowing the Senses to take charge.

As Lower Brain and his wife set off on their journey into the unknown, they carried with them the lessons of humility and selflessness that had shaped their reign. Their decision to willingly go into exile symbolized the transformation of their kingdom and its embrace of a future guided by principles like mindfulness, understanding and integrity.

King Lower Brains choice to recognize and honour the authority of the Senses while voluntarily stepping down from his throne marked the final chapter in the grand story of the Kingdom of Body. It served as a testament to the power of wisdom selflessness and paved the way, for a future characterized by balance and harmony under the leadership of the Senses.

Chapter 13: The Rise of Healing and Renewal

A. The Start of the Kingdom's Recovery and Revival

With the senses firmly established as the leaders of the Kingdom of Body and King Lower Brain, along with his wife voluntarily stepping aside, the process of healing and restoration commenced in full swing. Gradually, the wounds inflicted by the conflict between the senses and impulses began to fade, marking a new chapter in the kingdom's journey towards recovery.

The inhabitants of this realm, no longer under the influence of impulsive desires and chaos, experienced a newfound sense of well-being and stability. As balance returned to the Kingdom of Body, relief and gratitude filled their hearts while leaving behind burdens to embrace hope for a brighter future.

B. The Dedication of the Senses to Harmony, Equilibrium, and Enlightenment

Under the enlightened leadership of the senses, never before had prosperity thrived within the kingdom of the body. Their unwavering commitment to harmony, equilibrium, and enlightenment became guiding principles in their rule. They fostered an environment that cherished awareness, perception, and selfless action.

Recognizing that continuous self-improvement was vital for understanding their kingdom on a deeper level, they pursued knowledge about its inner mechanisms. They devoted themselves to the pursuit of knowledge and wisdom, drawing inspiration from consciousness and the lessons learned from the conflict.

Consequently, the Kingdom of the Body became a sanctuary for self-discovery and personal development. The residents were encouraged to explore their worlds, unleash their potential, and contribute to the well-being of the entire kingdom. The senses served as role models, embodying principles of equilibrium and moral integrity.

C. The Lasting Lessons Gained from the Conflict

The clash between the senses and the impulses left an imprint on the kingdom of the body but also imparted enduring teachings that would shape its future. The inhabitants grasped the consequences of desires and impulsive actions while recognizing the transformative power of self-awareness and mindfulness.

The conflict stood as a reminder of maintaining a balance within the kingdom while emphasizing vigilant self-governance. It underscored seeking guidance and spiritual wisdom during challenging times.

The Kingdom of the Body emerged from this conflict with heightened resilience and a profound appreciation for principles like balance and righteousness. The residents understood that ongoing commitment and self-discipline were essential on their journey towards recovery and enlightenment.

As the kingdom embarked on its path of healing and rebuilding, it did so with a sense of direction and a shared dedication to the principles of the senses. The lessons learned from the conflict served as a guiding light leading towards a future characterized by equilibrium, unity, and enlightenment.

The arrival of dawn symbolized the start of recovery in the Body Kingdom, marking the beginning of a chapter defined by the transformative influence of self-awareness and the timeless wisdom embodied in our senses.

Chapter 14; Conclusion

A. Reflecting on the Journey from Conflict to Recovery

As we look back on the journey that unfolded within the Kingdom of Body from the clash between the Senses and the Impulses to the emergence of healing and rejuvenation, we are reminded of the profound transformations that can take place in times of hardship.

The Kingdom of Body once plagued by disorder and imbalance discovered its path to healing and restoration through the wisdom and guidance provided by the Senses. The conflict acted as a crucible leading towards enlightenment and self-awareness.

B. The Lasting Impact of the Senses vs. Impulses Saga

The tale of the Senses versus Impulses left an enduring impact on the Kingdom of Body serving as a testament to the power of choice, accountability and inner wisdom. The kingdoms inhabitants learned that unchecked desires and impulsive actions could result in chaos and devastation while self-awareness and mindfulness could pave a path towards equilibrium and harmony.

The triumph of the Senses and subsequent transformation of the kingdom under their leadership became a moment in its history. It underscored how crucial it is to recognize one's nature while fulfilling responsibilities, with selflessness and integrity.

The story of the Senses vs. Impulses carries a message about the power of choice, responsibility and the importance of inner wisdom. It reminds us that we all face a battle, where we must decide between the path of recovery and the tempting shortcut towards chaos and destruction.

The Kingdom of Body serves as a metaphor for our world representing our higher faculties of awareness and perception through the Senses while our innate desires and impulses are symbolized by the Impulses. This conflict mirrors the struggle within our own hearts and minds.

Throughout their journey the Senses undergo a process of personal growth and spiritual evolution. They transition from being sensory perceptions to enlightened beings guided by Consciousness. This journey holds significance for those seeking to expand their own consciousness.

The initial step in their journey involves recognizing their limitations and understanding how their actions impact the Kingdom of Body. This self-awareness is crucial for their transformation as they strive to transcend these limitations and elevate their consciousness with guidance, from a source.

Reaching the realm of Consciousness, which symbolizes wisdom and enlightenment the Senses eagerly sought guidance and insight. In response Consciousness graciously imparted teachings on self-awareness the concept of Dharma and various spiritual paths. These teachings served as a roadmap for the Senses to elevate their consciousness and transcend their limitations.

Yet this journey was not about acquiring knowledge; it encompassed the practical application of that knowledge in everyday life. The Senses diligently practiced actions, mindfulness and self-discipline. Through effort and unwavering dedication, they gradually enhanced their consciousness.

One of the significant lessons learned by the Senses was the imperative to transcend ego and detachment from outcomes. Consciousness emphasized that true enlightenment arose from fulfilling one's duties without being attached to success or failure. This transformative concept liberated the Senses from the confines of desires driven by ego.

Interacting with Consciousness granted clarity of purpose, to the Senses. They comprehended that their responsibilities extended beyond gain; instead, they were intertwined with promoting the greater welfare of the Body Kingdom. This realization instilled within them a sense of direction and a higher calling.

The journey of our senses from perceiving the world around us to reaching a state of consciousness acts as a strong reminder that personal development and spiritual growth are within reach for those who are open, to self-awareness, wisdom and putting others before themselves. This journey is one of transformation and enlightenment guided by timeless principles that embody the essence of consciousness.

Story 4: Voyager's Journey into Ultimate Space

Between you and ultimate reality, just one veil
Remove it and before you, Nirvana unveils.
No more illusions, no more worldly tale
In that moment of clarity, Pure bliss prevails.

Chapter 1: The Prince's Unsettled Spirit

Deep within the boundaries of the Kingdom of the Body, a realm renowned for its peacefulness and flourishing communities, lived a prince named Voyager. This realm was celebrated far and wide for its abundance and serenity. However, what truly distinguished Voyager was not his lineage or opulence but rather the genuine compassion that radiated from his very core.

From his days, Voyager exhibited extraordinary kindness and empathy towards others. He possessed the ability to connect with the kingdom's populace, attentively listening to their joys and sorrows while readily extending a helping hand whenever necessary.

His compassionate demeanour endeared him to his subjects, who held him in high esteem.

Yet as he matured into adulthood, an inexplicable restlessness began to take hold of Voyager's spirit. This inner turmoil set him apart not only from his peers but also from those older than him within the kingdom. While others revelled in the beauty and tranquillity of their surroundings, Voyager's heart grew heavy with a realization—one that would forever alter the path he treads upon.

The sight of people enduring the hardships of life—old age, illness, and death—troubled Voyager deeply. He couldn't look away from the realities that all human beings face, regardless of their position or privilege. The understanding that even the happiest lives would eventually confront the challenges of mortality weighed heavily on his nature.

Voyagers' inner turmoil didn't stem from selfishness or a desire for gain. It arose from a wish to alleviate the suffering experienced by his fellow beings. His heart longed for a solution—a way to put an end to the pain and anguish he witnessed daily within the kingdom's walls.

As time went on, Voyagers internal restlessness grew more profound. The luxuries afforded by his status did not bring him comfort, nor could he ignore the suffering surrounding him. It felt as if an unyielding calling resonated within his soul—a demand for answers to life's most profound questions.

The people in the Kingdom of Body could perceive the turmoil in their prince's eyes, although they couldn't comprehend the depth of his inner struggle. Whispers began to circulate among the townsfolk, discussing Voyager's nature and speculating about what might befall their beloved prince.

Little did they realize that their compassionate leader was on the verge of embarking on an expedition, venturing far from the familiar comforts of the kingdom and delving into unexplored realms of existence. This relentless yearning that had weighed heavily upon him for so long would soon propel him towards a quest for enlightenment, a transformative journey wherein he would confront the very root of human suffering and strive to find solutions that surpassed the limitations of their world.

In the serenity of the kingdom's tranquil landscapes amidst rolling hills and breathtaking sunsets, Prince Voyager's destiny was being intricately woven, while an awe-inspiring adventure loomed on his horizon, poised to reshape not only his own life but also those around him.

Chapter 2: The Search for Freedom

As Prince Voyager grappled with his restlessness, his mind was not consumed by the pursuit of enlightenment. Instead, he was driven by a desire to find a remedy for the profound suffering that afflicted humanity within the Kingdom of the Body.

Even though the kingdom itself offered tranquillity and abundance, its relentless march spared no one. Witnessing the hardships of life—such as old age, sickness, and death—weighed heavily on Voyager's compassionate heart. He couldn't bear to see the suffering inflicted upon those he cherished dearly. This dissatisfaction with the human condition stirred his soul and fuelled his determination to seek answers.

With each passing day, as he roamed through the kingdom's landscapes and engaged in conversations with his subjects, the prince's unease only grew stronger. The stark contrast between his peaceful existence and the anguish faced by those burdened with mortality was impossible to ignore. The weight of their suffering bore down on him like a load.

It was during a poignant encounter that Voyager could no longer ignore the inner voice compelling him to find solutions. He ventured into the heart of the kingdom, visiting afflicted individuals in their homes. He gently grasped the hand of an elderly woman who had dedicated her life to working in the fields, now weakened in body and weary in spirit. As he looked into her eyes, he could sense the weight of a lifetime filled with struggles and hardships.

In spoken but profoundly wise words, she shared her own battles, fears, and aspirations. She longed for relief from the ceaseless suffering that had been her companion. Through her words, Voyager heard echoes of others who also bore the burden of such pain.

In that moment, an unwavering determination took hold within the prince's heart. He couldn't simply stand by while his people endured hardship. The inner voice that had whispered to him for years now transformed into a calling—a quest to discover a solution that would bring an end to the kingdom's anguish.

The decision to embark on this journey towards liberation was not made lightly. Voyager understood that it would take him away from the comforts of his royal life. He was fully aware that ahead lay a path riddled with challenges and uncertainties. He also knew that it was his duty to shoulder the weighty responsibilities of his kingdom.

However, the prince's deep empathy and unwavering resolve overshadowed any uncertainties or anxieties. He came to understand that his destiny extended beyond the boundaries of his kingdom; he was destined to confront the root cause of human suffering and find a solution that transcended their world's limitations.

With determination, Prince Voyager made a life-altering decision to embark on a journey for liberation, seeking answers that would bring an end to suffering. He could no longer ignore the pain tormenting his people. I was prepared to give up everything in pursuit of a higher truth.

Armed with a small bag filled with essentials and fuelled by an unwavering sense of purpose, Prince Voyager ventured once again into the unknown. His path now shone brightly, with the quest for liberation beckoning him onward towards the promise of ending suffering.

The road ahead would undoubtedly be fraught with challenges and trials. Voyager was fully prepared to face them head-on. The quest for liberation had become a driving force in his life, compelling him to seek profound answers that had haunted him throughout his existence.

As he delved deeper into the realms of existence, the prince's heart brimmed with purpose and unyielding determination. He no longer found satisfaction in existing within the boundaries of the kingdom. His desire for freedom had There was no going back. Voyager embarked on a journey that would take him to the core of existence itself—a path that would examine his resilience, question his convictions, and ultimately bring him into confrontation with the enigmatic resolution he yearned for.

Chapter 3: Leaving the Kingdom

Prince Voyager's preparations for his journey were thorough. Kept secret. He understood the seriousness of his quest. He took great care to ensure that no one knew about his departure until the day he left his loved ones and the kingdom behind.

In the quite hours of dawn, long before the sun cast its first rays upon the land, Voyager woke up silently. He knew it was time to venture into the unknown, determined to go without any disruptions or distractions.

With a heart, he gathered his supplies meticulously, choosing them carefully to sustain him on his challenging journey. His small bag held all that he needed. Provisions, spare clothes, and an unwavering determination to discover a solution that would end suffering.

As he moved through the palace, every step was cautious so as not to alert anyone of his departure. No one in the kingdom was aware of his plans since he had kept them hidden within himself, known only by him and the inner voice that compelled him to seek answers.

Outside the palace gates, a loyal charioteer awaited Voyager's arrival. The driver had been given the responsibility of accompanying the prince on this trip. With an understanding, Voyager got into the carriage, and they left the palace premises.

The driver skilfully guided the horses, avoiding travelled routes and any early riser's gaze. Their path took them into the heart of the kingdom, away from the landscapes that Voyager had known throughout his life.

As they dove deeper into territory, the first rays of dawn began to appear on the horizon. The soft, otherworldly glow illuminated their surroundings. Voyager observed the changing scenery with a mix of anticipation and determination.

The Kingdom of Body, asleep and unaware, remained oblivious to the prince's departure. He had left so early in the morning that no one had gotten a chance to stop him or say goodbye. His quest to find a solution for ending suffering was solitary; he knew himself and his inner calling, which urged him to seek answers.

The journey ahead was filled with uncertainty. Voyager was steadfast in his purpose. With every passing mile, he left behind the comforts of his life and stepped into an unknown realm. The road ahead of him was like a canvas ready to be painted with the adventures, obstacles, and discoveries that would shape his quest for freedom.

As the carriage moved forward into territory, Prince Voyager understood that he was starting a journey that would push his inner strength to its limits, question his beliefs, and eventually lead him to the answer he longed for. Leaving the kingdom behind marked the start of a transformation. One that would forever change his own life and the destiny of the Kingdom of Body.

Chapter 4: The Territory

As Prince Voyager delved deeper into unexplored landscapes, he encountered experiences that challenged his perception of the world. The landscapes he travelled through were Dreamlike, where the lines between reality and illusion became blurred and the concept of time itself became a mystery.

Motivated by his quest to find a solution to alleviate suffering, Voyager sought guidance from various spiritual schools. He approached them as a disciple, eager to learn and absorb their wisdom. Each school had its own distinct teachings and practices, and he approached them with an open mind and heart.

In his pursuit of answers, Voyager completed the teachings of the first spiritual school he joined. He dedicated himself wholeheartedly to their practices and principles in hopes of discovering the solution to ending suffering. However, despite his efforts, he found that the answers he sought remained out of reach.

Undeterred, Voyager proceeded to explore another school in search of different perspectives that might lead him closer to the desired revelation. He immersed himself in their teachings, absorbing their knowledge and wisdom with determination. Once again, the answers he sought eluded him.

For a decade, Voyager followed this pattern, going from one school to another in his relentless pursuit of finding a solution to end suffering. He remained committed and disciplined as a student, ready to explore every avenue in his search for enlightenment. However, no matter how determined he was, the answers continued to elude him.

Frustration slowly ate away at Voyager's determination. He had ventured through landscapes, delved deep into various spiritual practices, and sought guidance from revered teachers. Yet the ultimate answer remained veiled in mystery. It was a moment of reflection—a crossroads in his journey.

Finally, after years of seeking answers, Voyager made an important decision. He chose to embark on a journey within himself—to delve into the depths of his consciousness. He realized that the solution he sought might not be found in teachings or practices but rather within the hidden corners of his own existence.

With unwavering determination, Voyager revisited every technique he had learned throughout his voyage. He practiced each method with dedication, pushing himself to the point where even his physical form seemed to weaken. Despite these efforts, however, the answer he sought remained elusive—like a distant star on the horizon.

In the realm of his own mind, Voyager encountered the most profound inquiries about existence. He grappled with the intricacies of thought, the nature of suffering, and the elusive resolution that had compelled him on this grand expedition. The path he trod upon was treacherous, demanding not only physical stamina but also unwavering courage to confront the enigmas of his own being.

As he ventured deeper into the territory within himself, Voyager embarked on a journey that defied conventional comprehension. The landscapes he traversed were not rather realms of consciousness itself. The obstacles he faced were not rather intricacies woven into his very own thoughts.

With each step, Voyager drew nearer to unravelling the heart of the enigma that had driven him away from his realm. The answers he sought were not distant external pursuits but rather a profound exploration into his own awareness. It was a journey that would test both his endurance and determination to their limits, guiding him closer to the elusive solution he yearned for.

Chapter 5: The Revelation

After enduring six challenging years, Prince Voyager found himself on a solitary journey deep within his own being. Despite his determination and tireless practice of every technique he had mastered, the solution he sought remained elusive. This period was marked by solitude and introspection as he delved into the depths of his consciousness.

On a day, while standing at the edge of a calm stream, the weight of his journey bore down on him. His body, weakened by years of training, showed signs of fatigue.

At that moment, he faced a decision. To forge ahead or to succumb to the physical limitations imposed upon him.

Caught between the desire to push forward and the weariness threatening to overwhelm him, a moment of clarity washed over Prince Voyager. It was as if the stream before him held meaning—a symbol mirroring the challenges he had encountered along his quest.

In that instant, the prince caught a glimpse of what would later be known as the intricate barrier. It felt like the stream itself embodied a puzzle, reflecting the intricate maze of thoughts and emotions that had perplexed even the greatest thinkers throughout history.

The intricate barrier was unlike anything the prince had ever encountered. It wasn't an obstacle; rather, it mirrored the complexities and contradictions that define human existence. It served as a testament to the depths of human consciousness, presenting a challenge that transcended time and cultural boundaries.

The prince was no ordinary individual. His passion blazed like the sun, and in that moment of revelation, he made an unwavering vow. He pledged to overcome the barrier or face defeat in trying. This solemn commitment reverberated within him as he dedicated himself to unravelling mysteries that had eluded humanity for centuries.

With renewed determination, the prince pressed on with his journey, now armed with an understanding of the monumental task ahead. The intricate barrier stood as a representation of humanity's ultimate challenge. A reflection of its complex nature with all its contradictions. It presented a puzzle demanding his attention and an unwavering resolve to conquer it.

The revelation at the stream marked a moment in the prince's quest. It was a moment of understanding, a glimpse into the core of the puzzle he aimed to solve. The road ahead wouldn't be smooth. The obstacles he would encounter would push his endurance and determination to their limits. However, the prince remained undeterred because he had noticed the reflection of the obstacle in the stream. This made him realize that his journey had shifted decisively towards unravelling the mystery that had compelled him to leave behind his kingdom.

Chapter 6: The Ancient Wisdom

As the Prince persisted in his quest to overcome the intricate barrier that stood between him and the resolution of suffering, he delved deeply into the profound notion of "non-discrimination." This timeless wisdom would prove to be the key that would unlock the intricacies of the barrier and guide him towards his ultimate objective.

Non-discrimination wasn't a simple idea; it embodied an eternal and universal wisdom that transcended cultural boundaries and temporal limitations. It was a way of perceiving the world that went beyond sight. At its essence, non-discrimination entailed seeing past appearances and embracing life's paradoxes.

The prince understood that non-discrimination necessitated looking beyond surface-level observations and surpassing judgments and classifications that had coloured his perception of reality. It was an understanding that every aspect of existence, whether perceived as positive or negative, had a place within the vast tapestry of the universe.

In his pursuit of wisdom, the prince apprenticed under esteemed masters who had devoted their lives to unravelling life's complexities. He discovered that non-discrimination wasn't merely a concept but a profound truth demanding unwavering commitment and intense concentration.

The prince came to realize the significance of empathy as he delved deeper into the teachings of non-discrimination. To truly embrace this wisdom, he had to let go of his biases, prejudices, and preconceived notions. He needed to cultivate a sense of openness and compassion that enabled him to appreciate the beauty and importance of every aspect of existence.

Embracing paradoxes was another aspect of non-discrimination. The prince understood that life is filled with contradictions and complexities that cannot be neatly categorized or explained. Non-discrimination challenged him to confront these paradoxes and recognize how everything is interconnected.

Mastering non-discrimination was not a journey for the prince. He faced moments of struggle and doubt as he grappled with the depth of this wisdom. However, he persisted with unwavering determination because he knew that this knowledge held the key to overcoming the barriers that had eluded him for so long.

In his practice, the prince sharpened his concentration to a razor edge. He learned how to quieten the chaos of thoughts and distractions in his mind, allowing him to see things clearly. As each day went by, he delved deeper into the essence of treating everyone, finding the strength to confront his own inner thoughts and beliefs.

Treating everyone equally wasn't a philosophy to him; it became a way of living. It showed him the way through challenges and guided him towards his goal. With empathy in his heart, a willingness to embrace contradictions, and unwavering focus, the prince continued his journey, confident that he was on the path to unlocking the long-awaited secrets that had eluded him for so long.

Chapter 7: The Journey of Discovery

Guided by the wisdom of non-discrimination, the prince embarked on a profound exploration through the intricate layers of a complex barrier that separated him from finding a solution to end suffering. This expedition would lead him into the depths of his own consciousness, where he would confront personal demons and face challenges that would test his very essence.

With each step employing the tenets of non-discrimination, the prince gradually unveiled the multiple layers comprising this barrier, each representing a distinct aspect of human existence. These layers functioned like veils, obscuring the truth that awaited beyond. Undeterred by lurking shadows, he persevered in peeling one layer after another with unwavering determination.

Confronting demons became an everyday occurrence for the prince. The barrier seemed to materialize his fears, doubts, and insecurities—long-buried emotions rising to the surface. He stood firm in his resolve. Empathy and non-discrimination continued to guide him as he faced these adversaries head-on.

There were moments filled with apprehension and uncertainty when even reality itself came under scrutiny, as questioned by the prince. The barrier seemed difficult to overcome, and his own personal struggles weighed heavily on him. However, he remained steadfast in his belief in treating everyone well, knowing that it held the key to discovering the truth he desired.

His unwavering determination became a guiding light during the moments of his journey. The prince's faith in fairness and impartiality never wavered, carrying him through the most challenging trials. He recognized that the path to enlightenment wasn't smooth but rather filled with obstacles. Nevertheless, he pressed on with bravery and resolve because he understood that the knowledge, he gained would make every hardship worthwhile.

This quest for understanding wasn't simply physical; it was an exploration of the deepest corners of the prince's soul. He delved into his own consciousness, peeling away layers upon layers of conditioned beliefs and preconceived notions. With each layer shed, he grew closer to uncovering the truth that had eluded him for so long.

By practicing non-discrimination, the prince discovered how to see beyond illusions created by his mind. He realized that thoughts, feelings, and emotions were transient, like passing clouds without any worth. What really mattered was the essence that resided within.

The very core of his being Throughout his transformative journey, the prince uncovered a truth. practicing non-discrimination required unwavering focus. It demanded both braveries to confront life's mysteries and a willingness to embrace its paradoxes. Day by day, he grew stronger in his dedication, knowing he was inching closer to enlightenment.

This quest for discovery was not meant for the heart, but the prince was no ordinary individual. His steadfast belief in non-discrimination and his indomitable spirit carried him through the darkest moments. With each barrier he overcame, he drew nearer to the realm he yearned for. An end to suffering and boundless wisdom awaiting on the other side of complexities.

Chapter 8: The Triumph of Perseverance

Six years were dedicated to the relentless pursuit of the ultimate truth. The Prince's voyage through the barrier served as a testament to his unwavering determination and the unbreakable spirit that ignited within him. As he navigated through the currents of existence, he came to understand that the path towards enlightenment required sacrifices and profound transformations.

The prince made profound sacrifices along his journey. He had to let go of attachments that tied him down to illusions of the world. Material possessions and worldly desires held no power over him, as he recognized that true freedom lay in releasing the transient and embracing the eternal. He relinquished his ego, once a defining aspect of his identity, acknowledging its fragility as a construct of the mind.

These sacrifices were not without difficulty, demanding a level of detachment that few could comprehend. The prince had to confront his desires and face the shadows lurking within his consciousness. Moments of inner turmoil awaited him as he bid farewell to familiarity and ventured into uncharted territory.

Yet it was through these sacrifices that a critical turning point emerged in his journey. The intricate barrier that once appeared impenetrable began to fade away, uncovering a truth that had been elusive for a time. As he let go of his attachments and ego, he discovered the essence of his being—the core that surpassed the ups and downs of life.

The profound truth that emerged from his perseverance and determination was nothing but enlightenment. The prince stood face to face with what he had been searching for over years—nirvana, the end of suffering. It was a state of happiness and enlightenment, where joy didn't come from accumulating pleasures but from being free from suffering itself.

In that moment, he understood the truth that had evaded him for so long. True happiness doesn't lie in amassing pleasures but in liberating oneself from suffering. It was a revelation that deeply impacted him, filling his heart with joy. The prince triumphed over the barrier through non-discrimination and unwavering persistence—qualities that defined his journey.

The victory achieved through persistence wasn't just personal for the prince; it served as a testament to the resilience of the spirit. His journey serves as a reminder that extraordinary destinations often require arduous journeys. It served as a ray of hope for those who were looking to navigate life's maze in search of wisdom.

As the prince immersed himself in the glow of enlightenment, he realized that his journey was far from over. The pursuit of wisdom was an endeavour, an everlasting quest that extended into eternity. With a heart brimming with gratitude and a mind receptive to the possibilities of existence, he continued his exploration into the limitless realms of ultimate reality, forever striving to fathom the mysteries of the cosmos.

So, the tale of the prince, who embarked on a grand adventure to discover the solution to end suffering, reached a profound culmination. His expedition, characterized by intricacy, fervour, and an unwavering dedication to comprehending the essence of existence, illuminated the pathway towards Nirvana—the destination for all truth seekers.

Chapter 9: The Moment of Nirvana

After years of unwavering determination, the prince found himself standing at the edge of his aspiration— the experience of enlightenment, the cessation of suffering. It was a long-awaited moment that propelled him through the intricacies of obstacles and the trials within himself.

The Enlightenment was not an abstract idea; it represented a state of pure happiness and understanding that went beyond the confines of ordinary existence. As he entered this realm, the prince felt an overwhelming sense of tranquillity and liberation. It was as if a heavy burden had been lifted off his shoulders, allowing him to fully embrace the beauty of the universe.

In this state of enlightenment, the prince finally grasped a truth that had eluded him for so long. True happiness did not come from amassing material pleasures or pursuing desires. Instead, genuine happiness emerged from liberation itself—the freedom from suffering. This realization shook him to his core. He filled his heart with boundless joy.

As he immersed himself in the glow offered by enlightenment, a profound transformation swept over him. The weighty burdens from his past struggles encountered on his journey and the complexities posed by obstacles all faded into insignificance. He had surpassed the limitations imposed by the world. He transcended the boundaries of his own mind.

The impact of this realization on the prince was immeasurable. He had ventured into the depths of existence, confronted his fears, and unlocked ancient wisdom that embraced inclusivity. Now he stood on the threshold of enlightenment, a state that went beyond experiences and connected with the very essence of the universe.

In that moment of Nirvana, the prince comprehended that he had accomplished what he had sought for years. The solution to ending suffering was not found in pursuing desires or accumulating pleasures but in freeing himself from attachments and ego. This truth would forever shape his life as well as those who would follow in his footsteps. Finally, the prince returned to his home, where everything originated from staying there until his final breath.

The moment of nirvana marked the culmination of a journey for the prince—a journey characterized by complexity, passion, and an unwavering dedication to understanding existence. He had discovered the mysteries that had evaded humanity for ages, and his tale would serve as a timeless reminder that the pursuit of enlightenment's a worthwhile journey.

Filled with gratitude in his heart and guided by the wisdom of non-discrimination, the prince wholeheartedly embraced his state of being. He had arrived at his place, in Nirvana's ultimate realm, fully aware that he would forever be transformed.

Chapter 10: The Voyagers Enduring Legacy

The odyssey of the prince surpassed the limits of his own existence, turning into a timeless tale that would inspire countless generations. His story stood as a testament to the human spirit, driven by passion and guided by the wisdom of inclusivity. As his narrative echoed through history, it carried a message of hope and enlightenment for all those seeking to comprehend life's intricacies.

The impact left behind by the Voyager, as he came to be known, was one of lasting inspiration. His journey revealed that remarkable destinations often required enduring hardships. The princes unwavering determination and unwavering resolve became a guiding light for truth seekers—a reminder that embarking on the path towards enlightenment was an endeavour worth undertaking.

The timeless message of hope embedded in the Voyagers journey resonated with people from all walks of life. It spoke to humanity's capacity to transcend challenges and explore deeper truths beyond surface-level reality. The tale of the Voyager served as a reminder that pursuing knowledge and embarking on an inner transformation were noble pursuits capable of bringing profound insights and liberation from suffering.

Perhaps the most remarkable aspect of Voyager's lasting impact was its profound belief in "non-discrimination." This ancient wisdom guided him through the barrier that separated it from its ultimate destination. It transcended time and culture, offering a pathway to understanding existence.

The concept of non-discrimination, as comprehended by the prince, involved seeing beyond surface appearances. It required acknowledging that every facet of existence had a place in the vast tapestry of the universe. It demanded empathy for all living beings and a willingness to embrace life's paradoxes. This wisdom became a guiding principle for those seeking enlightenment, providing insights into the interconnectedness of all things.

In the Kingdom of Body, where the prince once resided, his legacy persisted as a symbol of hope and enlightenment. The kingdom's inhabitants revered him as a sage embodying humanity's potential for inner transformation. His story was passed down through generations, motivating individuals to embark on their personal journeys of self-discovery and spiritual growth.

Beyond the boundaries of the Kingdom of Body Voyagers, their influence spread far and wide. His story spread far and wide, reaching people from all backgrounds and cultures who sought a deeper understanding of life. The idea of treating everyone equally became a guiding principle for those who longed for peace and freedom.

As time passed, the impact of the Voyagers tale only grew stronger. It became a testament to the strength of the human spirit, the pursuit of wisdom, and the transformative power that lies within each person. The prince's legacy surpassed time and space, forever inspiring those who embarked on a journey to unravel life's complexities in search of enlightenment.

Thus, the Voyagers remarkable journey—filled with intricacies, passion, and an unwavering commitment to understanding existence—left a mark on the world. His legacy served as a reminder that seeking truth and embarking on a transformation are noble pursuits deserving our utmost dedication and perseverance. The enduring influence of the prince continues to shape the destinies of seekers as they navigate their own paths towards discovery and enlightenment.

Chapter 11: The Endless Quest

As the prince stood on the threshold of nirvana, he came to realize that his journey was far from reaching its end. The pursuit of enlightenment wasn't about arriving at a destination and then moving on; it embodied an eternal quest, an ongoing exploration of insight and the enigmas that lie within the universe.

The prince understood that the path to enlightenment wasn't a journey with a clear-cut destination. Rather, it encompassed a process of growth and self-discovery—an unending exploration of the limitless realms of existence. Guided by the wisdom of non-discrimination, he set forth on a phase of his expedition—one that extended infinitely into the horizon.

His exploration into self-realisation took him to depths he had never fathomed before. He dove into the intricacies of the mind, striving to unravel the mysteries entwined within thoughts, emotions, and perceptions. He questioned reality itself, seeking to understand how boundaries between oneself and the cosmos were constructed.

The prince's Quest was defined by curiosity and an unwavering dedication to grasping the essence of existence. He continued practicing non-discrimination fearlessly, embracing life's paradoxes with focus and determination. Each moment presented an opportunity for insight; each experience became a stepping stone along his path towards enlightenment.

As the prince contemplated the impact of his journey, he came to understand that it went beyond merely reaching a destination; it was a process of self-discovery and personal growth. The challenges, doubts, and moments of fear had all played their part in shaping him into a person of wisdom and empathy. He had surpassed the limitations of his ego and discovered a deeper connection with the world around him.

Reflecting on his journey, gratitude welled up within the prince's heart. He appreciated the obstacles that tested his determination, the moments of despair that fuelled his resolve, and the invaluable wisdom he gained along the way. While reaching his destination brought him joy, he also treasured every step taken on this transformative path.

Ultimately, the Prince's relentless pursuit wasn't about finding answers; it was a celebration of humanity's limitless potential. It served as a testament to how dedication, perseverance, and an unwavering quest for truth have power. Although he had arrived at Nirvana—the realm—he recognized that his journey would continue eternally.

As the Prince delved deeper into the realms of self-realisation and the enigmas of the universe, he embarked on this quest with a sense of awe and an unbounded curiosity. He realized that the true value lay in the journey itself, understanding that the pursuit of truth was a never-ending endeavour.

Chapter 12: The Ultimate Space

After a lifetime of exploration, the prince embarked on his voyage into a realm beyond the boundaries of ordinary existence. This moment held meaning as the culmination of years of relentless pursuit and unwavering determination.

As he entered this space, the prince experienced an indescribable sense of transcendence. It was as if he merged with the energy and wisdom of the universe, becoming one with the cosmos. Ego and self-vanished, replaced by a connection to all that existed.

The ultimate space was bliss and enlightenment, untainted by suffering. Here happiness arose not from seeking pleasures but from liberation itself—the freedom from suffering. The prince had reached the pinnacle of potential, a state few could comprehend.

In that moment of transcendence, the prince made a choice—he would never return. Having attained nirvana and life's mysteries, there was no need to re-enter a world entangled in suffering and attachment. His journey had reached its destination; he had discovered where he truly belonged.

The resolution of the story held significance. The prince successfully completed his quest, leaving behind a legacy that would stand the test of time. His journey was marked by complexity, passion, and an unwavering dedication to uncovering the essence of existence and shedding light on the path towards enlightenment.

The prince's legacy would continue to inspire generations. His story served as a timeless reminder that the pursuit of truth and inner transformation are noble pursuits deserving unwavering commitment and determination. His profound influence would shape the destinies of individuals, guiding them on their own journeys of self-discovery and enlightenment.

So as the prince embarked on his final voyage into uncharted realms, he did so with a heart brimming with gratitude and a mind open to the infinite possibilities in existence. While his personal journey had reached its conclusion, his enduring legacy would continue to shine brightly as a beacon of hope and enlightenment for all those who seek to unravel life's complexities.

Ultimately, Voyager had arrived at its destination in the boundless expanse of space, never to return. The prince story exemplified the transformative power embedded within the human spirit. An embodiment of wisdom-seeking endeavours and an unwavering quest for truth.

Story 5: How Brain and Mind Work

"In the depths of thought, Buddha dared to delve,
Where brain and mind their stories tell.
Through science he travelled, the mind's inner sea,
Unlocking the secrets of consciousness free."

Chapter 1: The Cognition of Birth – The Evolution of Cognitive Brain

In the mystic land of Nepal, a child was born—a child who would eventually become known as Buddha, the awakened one. Let's put aside the mystical aspect and delve into the fascinating journey of brain and mind that unfolded within this child, just as it does within each one of us.

Introduction to an Infant with a Developing Limbic System.

As young Siddhartha, his given name at birth, entered this world, his brain was brimming with potential. Like all newborns, his limbic system—often referred to as the centre—played a dominant role in shaping his early experiences. Emotions served as his language—an unadulterated expression of joy, fear, and curiosity. Through his system, he laid the groundwork for an emotional tapestry that would colour every aspect of his life.

Early Phases of Brain Development and Cognitive Growth:

During Siddhartha's few months on Earth, his brain embarked on an extraordinary voyage. Neurons sparked to life and forged connections, weaving a web that would support every thought and action he would take. His sensory encounters acted as brushstrokes that painted his understanding of the world around him. The vision of a lotus flower blooming gracefully; the touch of a breeze against his skin; the affection bestowed by his father—these experiences moulded and shaped his budding cognition.

Milestones in Cognitive Brain Evolution

As Siddhartha grew older, his cognitive abilities also developed. The prefrontal cortex, which is responsible for reasoning, planning, and decision-making, experienced milestones in its evolution. His first words, steps, and early curiosity about the world all marked significant progress in this development. The child was gradually transforming into someone capable of logical thinking and exploration.

With time passing, Siddhartha entered adulthood on the brink of maturity. His brain had undergone a transformation. The emotional turbulence of his years had given way to a more steady and rational thought process, facilitated by his cognitive brain. He began to question the world around him in search of answers to existential inquiries.

Unbeknownst to him, this was the beginning of his journey. The evolution of his mind and understanding of himself would lead him on a path towards enlightenment. As we delve deeper into exploring the workings of the brain and mind, Siddhartha's journey will serve as our guide.

On our journey to understand teachings, we trace the path of Siddhartha not as a god but as a representation of human capabilities. These abilities are deeply connected to how our brains have evolved and the mysteries that surround our minds. As we delve into his story, we will also delve into the discoveries that unveil the intricate workings of our inner selves, uncovering the significant influence of our brain and mind on shaping our very existence.

Chapter 2: Gautama's Journey Through Midlife Challenges

Introducing the Young Adult with a Developed Cognitive Brain:

Gautama possessed an extraordinary cognitive brain, like a finely tuned symphony of neurons and synapses.

His analytical abilities, planning skills, and decision-making precision were akin to those of a surgeon. However, there was something weighing heavily on his mind—a longing for connection. The absence of a mother's embrace had left an enduring mark on his soul.

Understanding the Importance of Building a Positive Self-Image: By nature, Gautama had a thoughtful disposition. He approached life with an attitude, even from a young age. Those who knew him recognized his resilience in facing challenges and his relentless pursuit of solutions with hope in his heart. Beneath this outward positivity lingered a profound yearning—a yearning for the connection he had never truly experienced. The absence of love had created an emptiness within him, leaving him longing for affirmation and a sense of wholeness.

Navigating the Shift from Cognitive Brain to Limbic Brain:

As life unfolded before Gautama's eyes, he encountered the realities of the world around him. The weight of responsibilities, societal expectations, and the unyielding passage of time began to take their toll. Different forms of stress, such as the pressures of being a leader or the expectations that come with adulthood, started to wear down Gautama's sharp cognitive abilities. At first, it was subtle and hard to notice, like a star slowly fading away.

As time went on, these stresses led to what we refer to as a midlife crisis. Gautama's strong cognitive abilities began to give way to the primal forces of his limbic system. Emotions surged uncontrollably like a river, while the calm waters of reason seemed far away. It was a period in his life when he felt adrift from his familiar sense of self.

The Emergence of the Subconscious Mind:

Amidst this turmoil, something remarkable started happening: Gautama's subconscious mind, which had long been hidden beneath the surface, began to emerge like the tip of an iceberg when the sea level dropped. This reservoir of forgotten memories, latent desires, and untapped potential came forward. He whispered ancient truths that he had long ignored.

So, what is this subconscious mind?

In terms, it's like the behind-the-scenes crew in a grand theatre production. It works tirelessly behind the scenes. Rarely steps into the spotlight. Deep within us lie our thoughts, emotions, memories, and automatic processes, eagerly waiting to leave their imprint on the stage of our experiences.

Have you ever wondered how this mysterious subconscious mind operates?

It's like a dance between nerves and hormones. When faced with prolonged stress, the nerves Key players in our parasympathetic nervous system. Can become obstructed. The excessive release of cortisol puts our bodies into gear, activating the sympathetic nervous system. Our hearts race while our primal brains take charge, and our cognitive brain takes a backseat. It is during these moments that the subconscious mind emerges to shape our thoughts and guide our actions.

Why is it important for us to comprehend this hidden force dwelling within us?

Because the subconscious mind, also known as the mind, is akin to a loyal yet passive companion, If we remain oblivious to its presence and influence, we risk becoming bystanders in our own lives. Trapped in a cycle of reactive responses. However, armed with understanding, we can become masters of our minds. We can tap into its intelligence and transform it into an empowering ally. A wellspring of insights and solutions that aid us in navigating life's intricate complexities.

As we delve into the depths of Gautama's life and explore the complexities of the brain and mind, let us not forget about the mind. It plays a crucial role in our journey of self-discovery, patiently waiting for us to realize its untapped potential.

Chapter 3: The Demise of the Cognitive Brain- The Emergence of Consciousness

I. Introduction

Gautama embarked on a quest that went beyond the boundaries of ordinary existence. His goal? To unravel the mystery behind suffering and, in doing so, free humanity from its constraints.

This was no ordinary journey. It was an expedition that would test endurance, a pilgrimage that would take Gautama to the very edge between life and death. As he dove deeper into the enigmas of existence, his quest took a turn, immersing him in the depths of his own consciousness.

II. A Decade of Exploration

Gautama's pursuit of truth led him on a remarkable adventure through diverse landscapes of wisdom and knowledge. For ten years, he explored ancient teachings, absorbed the wisdom imparted by numerous mentors, and delved into various techniques and schools of thought.

Throughout this period, Gautama left no stone unturned. He ventured into the revered realms where philosophers dwelled, engaging in debates and absorbing the tapestry woven by their profound ideas. He humbly sat at the feet of gurus, eagerly soaking up their teachings like a sponge.

His relentless pursuit of knowledge was driven by curiosity and a deep desire to understand the nature of human suffering. Gautama dedicated himself to exploring the intricacies of meditation, delving into the depths of mindfulness, and immersing himself in the practices of ascetics. He faced challenges along his path, experiencing moments of doubt, frustration, and the constant presence of suffering itself. However, he remained determined and resolute in his quest.

As he delved deeper into this realm of wisdom, Gautama's understanding expanded. He began to recognize the threads that connected different aspects of human wisdom. Yet despite his progress, finding a solution to end suffering remained elusive—like a mirage on the distant horizon.

III. Reflection in Solitude

After a decade filled with exploration, Gautama embarked on a solitary voyage that would lead him straight into the essence of his being. For six years, he sought solace in the wilderness, far away from the distractions of society and deeply embraced by the beauty of nature.

During this time, Gautama's physical and mental well-being underwent a change. The demands of contemplation pushed him to his limits as a human being. His strong physique grew weak, his garments turned tattered, and the marks of hardship etched themselves onto his face.

As the external world became distant and obscure, an extraordinary internal transformation occurred. Gautama's higher brain, where thought and intellect reside, began to yield its dominance. It was as if the very essence of his existence was undergoing a metamorphosis.

In this crucible of seclusion, Gautama's consciousness experienced an evolution. His higher brain, which had guided him for years in exploration and understanding, now took a backseat. In its place surged the instincts of his lower brain—a dormant force awakened.

This transition marked a point in Gautama's journey—a shift from the complexities of intellectual pursuit to a more instinctual state of existence. It felt like he had regressed from being highly intelligent to a state of simplicity similar to that of a baby, but with the wisdom and knowledge accumulated over a lifetime.

However, despite his mental decline, Gautama's determination remained steadfast. He didn't venture into the wilderness to escape the world but to confront the depths of his own mind.

IV. The Awakening of Consciousness

In the solitude of the untamed landscapes, Gautama's consciousness underwent an immensely significant transformation. It was as if the floodgates of his world burst open, flooding him with an overwhelming torrent of personal experiences.

These experiences were unlike anything he had ever encountered before—they were raw, unfiltered, and deeply intimate. It appears Gautama had tapped into the core of existence itself. Sensations, emotions, and thoughts swirled within him, each one competing for his attention.

Amidst this deluge of personal experiences, a dichotomy emerged—a fundamental battle within his consciousness. On one hand, there were longings. Those raw instinctual urges were enticed by their alluring charm. They softly whispered of the satisfaction of surrendering to carnal pleasures and of indulging in fleeting worldly delights.

On the other hand, there was the voice of virtue, normality, and the pursuit of a loftier ideal. It encouraged Gautama to resist the allure of impulses, embrace a path grounded in discipline, and strive for a state of existence that transcended the fleeting desires of the present moment.

The clash between these opposing forces was nothing grand. It was a battle fought within the very essence of his being. A struggle that threatened to engulf him entirely. The impulsive longings relentlessly pulled at him, promising pleasure but ultimately leading to suffering. Meanwhile, righteousness and normalcy beckoned with the promise of a path towards healing and transcendence.

It was within this crucible of conflict that Gautama began gaining profound insights into the workings of his physical and psychological makeup. Along with something enigmatic known as 'ether.' Everything began falling into place like cosmic puzzle pieces coming.

Yet even with this newfound understanding There was still one enigmatic piece that eluded Gautama. The ultimate resolution is to alleviate suffering. Although Gautama had glimpsed into the depths of his consciousness, the pursuit of ending suffering continued to elude him.

V: Unravelling the True Cause of Suffering

As the tumultuous waves of experiences continued to collide within Gautama's mind amidst the inner struggle between desires and ideals, a moment of profound clarity emerged. It was as if a celestial light had illuminated the corners of his thoughts, revealing a truth that had escaped humanity for countless generations.

In that instant, Gautama comprehended the fundamental root cause of suffering itself. He perceived with clarity that suffering was not an arbitrary affliction but an inherent aspect of our human existence. It was interwoven into the fabric of life as an inescapable consequence arising from our relentless pursuit of desires and attachments.

Gautama realized that suffering originated from our ceaseless yearning for things to be different than they're. It stemmed from our attachment to pleasures and avoidance of pain, which kept us ensnared in an endless cycle of anguish. However, despite this revelation, the elusive solution to end suffering remained just beyond his grasp. Gautama had an insight into the underlying cause, but the path to liberation remained mysterious. The realization of the root cause of suffering was a moment in Gautama's journey. It was a point where everything started to make sense except for the ultimate objective of ending human suffering.

VI: The Journey Continues

With this profound understanding of the origin of suffering etched in his mind, Gautama's journey was far from complete. The solution to end suffering remained elusive, like a captivating mirage beyond his reach.

Undeterred by the complexity of the task, Gautama embarked on a struggle—a relentless pursuit to unravel the secret behind freeing oneself from suffering. It was an expedition that would test his endurance, challenge his intellect, and demand unwavering determination.

The awakening of consciousness marked a turning point in Gautama's quest. It was a moment when subjective experiences flooded in. Desires clashed with ideals at their peak. It was also when he uncovered the root cause of suffering—a moment filled with clarity and a glimpse into how his own mind and the world operated.

Chapter 4: The Journey Towards the Ultimate Source

In Gautama's quest for knowledge, he reached a crucial realization: the only thing holding him back from finding a way to end suffering was his own mind. It felt as if his consciousness itself had become the frontier to explore. To overcome this obstacle, he employed a technique rooted in scientific principles called "non-discrimination."

The practice of "non-discrimination" involved a systematic approach to understanding his own mind. Gautama carefully examined the layers of his consciousness, delving into the experiences, thoughts, and emotions that kept him trapped in the cycle of suffering.

Through observation and introspection, he made an incredibly profound discovery. It was a scientific breakthrough—the realization that suffering arises from our constant tendency to differentiate between pleasant and unpleasant experiences. This process of discrimination lies at the heart of suffering, perpetuating an endless cycle of attachment and aversion.

Gautama's understanding was grounded in scientific terms. He recognized that, through its cognitive processes, the human mind had constructed a world full of suffering. The "solution" lay in deconstructing this self-created reality.

As Gautama delved into the complexities of his own consciousness, he experienced a moment of enlightenment that resembled a significant scientific breakthrough. It dawned on him that the key to ending suffering wasn't some revelation but rather a profound comprehension of the mind's nature itself.

Armed with this understanding, Gautama broke free from the chains of suffering. It was the truth he had been seeking all along. An empirical grasp of the human condition went beyond religious doctrines and restrictions.

Gautama's journey reached its peak as he embraced this truth. His path wasn't one driven by spirituality or mysticism but by a scientific exploration into the inner workings of the human mind. With suffering eradicated, he experienced a sense of serenity, akin to Nirvana. A state liberated from tormenting attachments and aversions.

Thus, Gautama's journey, rooted in scientific terms, culminated in success. It was an expedition that unravelled the enigmas of the mind and illuminated the pathway to liberation from suffering.

The End

Notes

Notes

Notes

Printed in Great Britain
by Amazon